THE CENTRAL SCHOOL OF
SPEECH AND DRAMA

UNIVERSITY OF LONDON

SHIRE PUBLICATIONS LTD

ABOUT THE AUTHOR

Pat Earnshaw has been a keen collector of lace for a number of years. She is a member of the Lace Guild, the International Old Lacers and the Costume Society. She worked as a consultant in the lace department at Phillips Auction Rooms, Bond Street, London, when their textile sales were started in 1973. Currently she is in charge of the textile department at Harrods Auction Galleries, Barnes, and a lecturer on the identification of lace at the English Lace School at Tiverton. She valued the impressive collection of Dr Arthur Spriggs, which is on loan to the English Lace School, and also catalogued the lace for the Honiton and Allhallows Museum.

ACKNOWLEDGEMENTS

My most grateful thanks are due to Ronald Brown for his excellent' photographs, which so effectively convey the visual content of the lace itself. All the illustrations are by him, except for: figs. 2-5, by courtesy of the National Portrait Gallery, London; figs. 1, 19, 45 and 55, taken by John Yallop, by courtesy of the Honiton and Allhallows Museum; figs. 6, 7, 8, 10, 14, 15, 20, 47, 49, 50, 57, 68, 69, 70, 72, 76, 77, 78, 82, 90, 93, 96, 100, 105, 107, 108, 112, 117, 119, 127, 128, 133, 155, 157, 158, 161 by Peter Mann and Alastair Thompson.

I am also indebted to the following for kindly allowing photographs of their lace to be taken: the Joslyn Baker collection, for figs. 7, 8 and 37; Mary Chugg, Eileen Cooper Antiques, Braunton, Devon, for fig. 44; the Textile Conservation Centre, Hampton Court Palace (Reference Collection), for fig. 134; Esther Beeson's museum, for fig. 147.

I am deeply appreciative of the invaluable advice and criticism given by Santina Levey of the Victoria and Albert Museum, London; and of Jeremy Farrell's civility in showing me the collection of machine-made laces at the Nottingham Costume Museum.

The quotations on page 20 from Queen Victoria's Journal are by gracious permission of Her Majesty The Queen.

The cover design is by Ron Shaddock. The two pieces of lace which appear on the cover are shown in figs. 48 and 95.

Note. The measurements given in the captions to the photographs refer, unless otherwise stated, to the longest axis of the illustration.

Set in 10 on 11 point English roman and printed in Great Britain by C. I. Thomas & Sons (Haverfordwest) Ltd, Press Buildings, Merlins Bridge, Haverfordwest.

CONTENTS

1. A royal warrant appointing Amy Lathy maker of thread lace to Queen Adelaide, 1830.

2. Henry, Prince of Wales, by R. Reeke. c. 1610. Note the ruffs and cuffs edged with punto in aria, and the fashionable shoe roses.

A CHRONICLE OF LACE

Before embarking on the story of the development of lace as a decoration for costume and household goods it would be helpful to define what lace is. The word 'lace' is derived from the Latin *laqueus* meaning a noose, a noose being a hole outlined by a rope, string or thread. So the term 'lace' covers all that great variety of ornamental openwork fabrics formed by the looping, plaiting, twisting or knotting of the threads of flax, silk, gold, silver, cotton, mohair or aloe, whether done by hand or by machine. A simplified, but still valid, definition would be that lace is 'a lot of holes surrounded with thread'.

Rather strangely, although thread and fabric go back to prehistoric times and embroidery and patterned weaving almost as far, there is little evidence of the existence of lace itself before the end of the sixteenth century, apart from slender references to crochet and a kind of network in the time of Edward III (1312-77). 'Laces' as recorded in fifteenth-century manuscripts appears to refer to boot or shoe laces or to braids; and gold and silver laces which archaeologists claim to have found, from earlier times, may be simply pieces of embroidery from which the cloth they were worked on has rotted away. Strangely also, lace in its rich variety appears to be a European phenomenon only, and no lace developments occurred in the other five continents.

Lace as we know it began in the sixteenth century as a decoration on handspun and handwoven linen, little more than a form of embroidery that consisted of making holes, either by removing threads or by gathering them together in groups (drawn and pulled threadwork, known as *punto tirato*), or by cutwork, where holes were cut in the material and then embroidered around *(punto tagliato)*. These laces are known to have been made in Venice, France and Spain, and their use was mainly ecclesiastical, as in altar cloths and alb flounces.

An extension of the thread-drawing technique was the progressive removal of threads to leave only a square or rectangular frame. Within this frame diagonals were constructed and then some of the spaces were filled in with buttonhole stitches in an almost unlimited variety of patterns, producing a much more elaborate and sophisticated lace known as reticella, with some solidly worked parts and some more open. The characteristic of reticella was the skeleton of linen thread which remained to support the buttonhole-stitch fillings.

At this point a step was taken which finally distinguished lace from a form of openwork embroidery. The woven linen material was dispensed with and the lace was made 'out of the air', that is by the enclosure of spaces by threads. So it was called punto in aria (stitches in air). First a design was drawn on parchment and major guide threads were laid down to form the outline of the pattern; then around and within these guide threads thousands and thousands of tiny buttonhole stitches were worked and built up out of fine thread into a beautiful fabric of lace.

In the early years of its production punto in aria preserved the angular or circular devices of geometric design to which punto tirato and punto tagliato had of necessity been limited by the warp and weft of the linen material. Punto in aria has been found on early albs, but by the late sixteenth century it also had secular use in the ruffs and cuffs of the Elizabethan and early Stuart periods. In the time of James I (1566-1625) 25 yards (23 metres) of fine lace were required to edge a ruff. Venetian pattern books, for example one by Vinciolo dated 1587, still exist showing the range of geometric designs then in use — and also some non-geometric, for the freedom from the longitudinal and horizontal weave of the linen was soon to release the imagination of the designers in flowing patterns of scrolls, cherubs, courtiers, flowers, pagodas, heraldic devices and cornucopia, producing an amazing richness of beauty in softly textured thread of exquisite fineness, which reached its pinnacle in the first half of the eighteenth century.

Punto in aria was a needlepoint lace, worked entirely in buttonhole stitch over a parchment base often fixed to a pillow. (Since other types of lace were also worked on pillows the term 'pillow lace' is ambiguous and better avoided.) In the sixteenth and seventeenth centuries Italy was the leader in the production of needlepoint laces, the most famous being the Gros Point de Venise, a very heavy lace with huge scrolls like carved ivory, at its peak between 1620 and 1650; its diminished but perhaps prettier counterpart Rose Point; and finer still the delicate Point de Neige with tier upon tier of prickly spikes like snow crystals, the motifs linked by frivolously decorated brides, at its peak between 1650 and 1700.

So far I have not even mentioned the lace which today is the type most heard about: bobbin lace. While needlepoint was a derivative of embroidery, bobbin lace was a derivative of weaving. It is possible to argue that bobbin preceded needlepoint, or needlepoint bobbin, but it is a futile exercise. Both laces were in fashion in the early seventeenth century, adorning the Stuart kings. Their superb quality was fully appreciated by the nobility of the period, who valued them at their true worth more highly than jewels or silks, knowing the endless hours of slow painstaking labour in highly uncomfortable cow byres, where the moist warmth emanating from the cows below kept the fine flax thread supple and the hands of the lacemakers from becoming stiff with cold. Some workers made only 24 inches (600 millimetres) in a whole year, and as many as 1,200 bobbins might be needed to make a wide flounce which would progress at no more than an inch (25 millimetres) a day. Charles I is known to have spent

3. Lady M. Scudamore, by M. Gheeraedts, c.1614. The ruff is plain linen; the cap and cuffs are decorated with cutwork/reticella and punto in aria.

£1,000 in 1625 on his personal lace and linen, and in 1633 £1,500, in the currency of those days. In 1638 a pair of shoe 'roses' in metal lace could cost £30. Bobbin lace was recorded in 1612 at 9 shillings a yard (0.9 metres), 150 yards (137 metres) being used in a royal marriage wardrobe, as well as 1,692 ounces (48 kilograms) of silver bone lace.

The early ecclesiastical lace was subject to only slight variations of design, and its use in England had been largely suppressed by the Reformation of the sixteenth century. Secular lace, however, was subject to the vagaries of fashion. It was a change in the style of the neck decoration from ruffs to collars, as in Van Dyck's portraits, which began the rise in popularity of bobbin lace as opposed to needlepoint. During the first quarter of the seventeenth century the stiffly starched linen of the ruff, edged with punto in aria, gave place to low flat collars of soft pliable bobbin lace, mainly Dutch and Flemish, made of the exceptionally fine flax thread of northern Europe which for more than 150 years has never been repeated, perhaps because some change in climatic conditions affected the sturdiness of the flax plant or caused a particular variety of that species, *Linum usitatissimum*, to die out. This might easily happen as it is an annual plant reproduced by seeds alone. Also the cultivation of the plant for its thread must have become less profitable to the growers after the invention in 1792 of the cotton gin, which made cotton a much cheaper fibre for woven fabrics.

The relative cheapness of bobbin lace compared with needlepoint favoured its development. The early bobbin laces had a solid woven appearance, the design being to some extent geometric in imitation of the fashionable needlepoints which they were replacing. At first the edges were scalloped; then the scallops were filled in to give a straight edge and the motifs, or *toile*, of the design became slightly separated by a suggestion of background mesh, or *reseau*.

In the early seventeenth century bobbin lace was made mainly in northern Europe, in particular Flanders, while needlepoint was made mainly in southern Europe, in Venice. However, by the mid seventeenth century Genoa and Milan in the south were producing bobbin laces which rivalled those of Flanders; and Flanders in return was producing needlepoint lace, though never in large enough quantities or sufficiently spectacular to provide any serious competition with that of Venice.

Both bobbin and needlepoint laces were imported into England with the result that the English laces suffered. In 1621 an office was set up to promote home industry and to levy a tax on luxuries. In 1635, in the reign of Charles I, the import of foreign laces other than gold and silver was prohibited and the melting down of gold and silver coinage to make lace thread in England was disallowed. But the rich were addicted to the Flemish and Italian laces and a long period of smuggling followed.

4. Sir Arthur Capel and family, by Cornelius Johnson, c. 1640. Hair is worn longer, and the ruff has given way to the flat soft linen collar, edged with scalloped Flemish lace.

During the Commonwealth, 1649-60, the wearing of gold and silver laces, cuffs, fine collars, gartering and shoe roses was forbidden under Puritan rule. Nevertheless when Cromwell died his body was most gorgeously attired, more lavishly than that of a dead king, in purple velvet, ermine and the richest Flemish laces, showing that, like some people today, he had no objection to wealth and finery in themselves, only to other people possessing them. The throat decoration known as a gorget or whisk in 1660 cost £50.

Following the Restoration, Charles II in 1662 passed a further act of Parliament prohibiting the import of foreign laces. Any lace discovered being smuggled through the customs was to be forfeited, and a fine of £100 paid. Charles, however, regarded himself as above the law and in the same year ordered quantities of foreign lace for his family. He is known to have paid £194 for three cravats of Point de Venise and 24 shillings a yard for 57 yards (52 metres) of 'point' to trim his ruffles. Spanish needlepoint was also popular, being a close copy of the Venetian.

When the flowing wig became fashionable about this time the flat collars were hidden beneath hair, so they were replaced by the cravat, which showed the lace clearly beneath the chin. While the men garnished themselves with wildly expensive broad pieces of lace, 9 inches (230 millimetres) deep, it became the custom, according to Samuel Pepys (1633-1703), for ladies more modestly to trim their petticoats with a gimp lace of their own making. This was constructed from thick black or white silk, or from metal thread, wound around cord and plaited or twisted into a kind of braid, without the use of bobbins or needle.

Contemporary with the cravat were large handkerchieves edged with lace and lace-trimmed gloves and aprons. These were so coveted that they attracted the attention of thieves, and the newspapers of the time were full of reports of losses of lace and offers of rewards. There are records also of fans of Flemish lace during the Carolean period, and of lace-trimmed nightcaps, or toquets, in which it was court etiquette for royalty to die.

In 1698, during the reign of William of Orange, yet another act was passed prohibiting the importation of lace. The penalty was now fixed at a fine of £1 per yard (0.9 metres), plus confiscation. Flanders retaliated by prohibiting the importation of English wool, valued at several hundred thousand pounds a year, and this caused such distress in England that the law was repealed in 1699.

At the beginning of the eighteenth century came the period of the fontange, the lappets, the engageants, the frills and flounces of female dress — 'every part of the garment in curl like a Friesland hen', someone wrote in the *Spectator*. Expenditure on lace became even greater than in Stuart times. Queen Mary in 1694 spent £1,918 in the currency of the day. The cost of lace at that time seems staggering to us only because today lace is so grossly undervalued. In terms of the hours spent in making it, the lace workers were still, then, very poorly paid.

Among Queen Mary's purchases were 16 yards (15 metres) of lace for two toilets at £12, £192; an apron of lace, £17; 24 yards (22 metres) to edge six handkerchieves at £4 10s a yard, £108. King William in 1695 surpassed his wife and achieved a total of £2,459 19s. This included six point cravats, £158; 54 yards (49 metres) for barbing cloths, £270; 117 yards (107 metres) of cutwork for trimming twelve handkerchieves, £485 14s 3d; 78 yards (71 metres) for 24 cravats at £8 10s, £663. It is uncertain what kind of lace these accounts refer to, but there appears to have been sufficient patronage of English laces for them to prosper greatly and Defoe, about 1724, quoted the price of Blandford, Dorset, lace as £30 a yard. Be that as it may, the wax images of William and Mary in Westminster Abbey show both of them wearing Venetian Point.

Soldiers at this time had not only to fight but also to appear elegant, and they went into battle wearing silk stockings and lace cravats. A contemporary publication, *The World*, regretted this as an appalling waste of finery, as it could not be recovered when they were killed.

Pickpockets and other thieves went for lace rather than jewels since

5. Prince James, the Old Pretender, and his sister Louise, by Nicholas de Largilliére, 1695. The princess wears a fontange, stomacher, cuffs and apron of a French needlepoint, probably point de France. As fussier styles are in fashion the lace becomes softer and can be gathered.

many of the eighteenth-century jewels were made of paste, while the fabulous handmade laces were of enormous value and much coveted. Thieves were known to slit open the leather backs of hack coaches and take the lady's 'head'. This was less alarming than it sounds, for the term referred to the wig with its lacy superstructure of fontange and lappets. In an effort to stamp out this crime the police requested all ladies to sit in the carriages with their backs to the horses. Lace became a form of currency, being used to raise money to support the Old and Young Pretenders, especially during the almost successful Jacobite rising of 1745; it was also bartered for the newly fashionable Chinese export porcelain.

During the reign of Queen Anne (1704-14) the simple 'Flemish' of the seventeenth century developed into the bobbin laces of Binche — the forerunner of Valenciennes, Mechlin and a type of guipure sometimes confusingly called Point d'Angleterre. The French needlepoints of Alençon and Argentan were also much worn. These had been started by Colbert at the town of Alençon in 1665. They had a greater lightness of texture than the Venetian laces and more flexibility of design, so that they gradually replaced them in the world of fashion and brought about their decline.

The laces of the seventeenth century had been bold, beautiful and ostentatious, the most visible proof of the wealth of the wearer. The eighteenth-century laces, in contrast, were gossamer-fine, needing a magnifying glass to reveal the splendour of their workmanship and design. To make up for this they were worn in vast quantities, particularly by women, though cuffs and cravats of one sort or another were still favoured by men.

It was during William III's reign, in 1685, that Louis XIV's persecution of the Huguenots caused lace workers to flee from France to England. This led to a great improvement in English lace during the eighteenth century, and while needlepoint, especially Spanish, remained a necessity for court wear, bobbin laces held the field. Buckingham lace is known to have been well established at this time, adapted from the laces of Lille and Mechlin.

The fontange of lace, which had become so high and elaborate as to appear quite ridiculous, went out of fashion by about 1710, but lace remained a mania for all who could afford it, or indeed who could not, for many socialites owed hundreds or thousands of pounds to their lace merchants.

During the reign of George II (1727-60) Flemish lace was highly fashionable. However, the king did what he could to encourage British manufacture. At his eldest son's marriage in 1736 the bride was decked entirely in English laces. Ladies were also encouraged to 'buy British' in order to give livelihood to the poor, and in 1750 the Society of Anti-

6. An example of the non-geometric designs of the eighteenth century. Part of a point d'Angleterre lappet, bobbin lace, droschel reseau, c. 1750. (200 mm.)

Gallicans was founded which gave prizes for goods of English manufacture, including lace. Towards the end of George II's reign silk lace was beginning to appear and was generally known as *blonde*, but apart from this lace was still made of flax thread. Aprons edged with lace remained fashionable and might cost as much as 200 guineas.

Throughout the eighteenth century, because of the various acts prohibiting the importation of foreign laces, especially the needlepoints of France, Spain and Venice, smuggling was rife. By the middle of the century the customs officials had become very strict and exercised the right to search people's houses and ask them to account for any foreign lace found there. They also invaded tailors' shops and confiscated any apparel or material made abroad. The confiscated lace was burnt, a shameful loss of unrepeatable artistry.

George III (reigned 1760-1820) extended his father's work in protecting English manufactures. In 1764, for example, he ordered that all the lace to be worn at the wedding of his daughter Augusta was to be English. It was the intention of the noble lady guests to disregard this order, but three days before the marriage the customs officials descended on the court milliner and carried away all the foreign finery. In the same year there was a seizure of not less than 100 pounds (45 kilograms) of French lace, all of which was burnt. Yet the attempts continued: lace was hidden in loaves, in turbans, in books, around babies, in umbrellas. Coffins were a somewhat repetitious hiding place, having been tried with success in George II's reign when the coffin of Bishop Atterbury, brought home from France, contained with the corpse £6,000 worth of French lace. Less successful had been the coffin of a clergyman opened by customs during the first quarter of the century and found to contain only the cut-off head, hands and feet, the body having been replaced by a sackful of Flemish lace of almost astronomical value.

These smuggling attempts continued into the nineteenth century, and Mrs Palliser herself records her frantic concern to find a safe hiding place for a Brussels veil for which she had paid 100 guineas. Having suspected people around her of being spies, she eventually had it stitched into the waistcoat lining of an MP who was travelling in her party so that it fitted into the hollow of his back and was not discovered.

While confiscated lace was burnt, much exquisite irreplaceable lace was also lost by burial, it being the custom for corpses to be decked out in their smartest clothes.

The glorious era of lace ended contemporaneously with the French Revolution of 1789. Gowns were suddenly utterly simple, of fine India muslin or silk gauze, untrimmed except for trifles of blonde lace or white embroidery. Lace was out, except for state occasions, and people became puritanical about its expense and its frivolity. Large collections were cast out by families to their waiting maids as if they were rubbish, thus demonstrating how absurdly fashion can triumph over artistic appreciation. Fear of death may also have played some part in this destruction: lace was associated with aristocrats, and aristocrats with the guillotine. Much of this cast-off lace was inevitably wasted by deterioration or by cutting up and wearing out, but still much was recovered later from farmhouses and theatrical wardrobes when a taste for lace began to revive during the nineteenth century, and lace collections began to be assembled. The old pieces came to be worn again, but often with a mixture of types and in poor taste so that their true beauty did

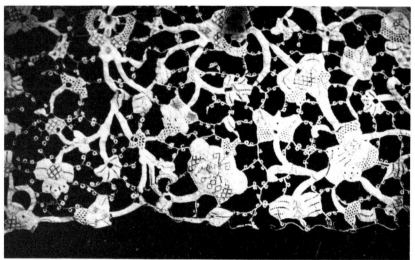

7. English needlepoint dated 1689. This needlepoint is very similar to Venetian point plat but typically of coarser thread and workmanship and of a disjointed design. (160 mm.)

not appear. Cannibalisation of lace during the nineteenth century was also common: flounces were turned into berthas or shawl collars and priceless lappets into dress trimmings or jabots. While the old was thus bit by bit frittered away there was nothing new, of equivalent quality, to replace it.

Lace revivals were attempted in many places, not only to resurrect an art form, but to give employment to needy women and children, for example in Malta by Lady Hamilton Chichester in 1833, in France by Napoleon I and later by the Empress Eugenie, wife of Napoleon III (married 1853), in England by Queen Adelaide, wife of William IV (married 1818), and also in Ireland and Madeira. These revivals were mainly between 1840 and 1890 and produced some magnificent individual works of art but nothing that was both good and economic to produce on a commercial scale, for in the nineteenth century handmade lace had a ruthless rival to contend with, the rapidly developing machine laces.

Machine lace was a product of the industrial revolution, which so much affected the textile industry during the mid eighteenth century. A net made on the Stocking Frame first appeared about 1764. This used one continuous thread to make a looped fabric and so had a tendency to unravel, rather like knitting. Improvements followed with the square net (1777-1830) and the point net with a hexagonal mesh (1780-1820), and by 1830 there were diamond-shape meshes giving the net a lighter, more airy appearance. The machines producing these nets were the Warp Frame, invented in 1775; the Bobbin Net machine of John Heathcoat in 1808; the

Pusher in 1812; and the Levers in 1813. In 1816 Heathcoat's mill in Loughborough was attacked by the Luddites, who championed the cause of those workers who had been made redundant by the new-fangled machinery, and his fifty-five lace frames were destroyed. He subsequently moved to Tiverton in Devon and by 1851 had no fewer than three hundred machines making plain silk net. The factory which he set up there still exists today, the machines producing nylon, silk and elastic nets. Silk net, or tulle, for embroidery was also produced in France, for example in Lyons, from the 1820s. In 1823 Heathcoat's patent expired, and Nottingham became the scene of a fury of invention and production.

The next step was to make patterned laces. The early nets were often embroidered by hand in darning stitch (needlerun) or chainstitch (tambour work), but as early as 1825 the Pusher machine had been adapted to make bullet-hole net. In 1831 spotted net was made using a circular comb machine, and by the 1840s there were good imitations of many of the handmade laces, in particular almost undetectable copies of simple Valenciennes, Mechlin and Bucks. This patterning was greatly helped by the invention in France of the Jacquard system. This had been patented in 1805, and its object was to mechanise the manipulation of the threads which made the design — in woven materials in the first instance. The attachment to the looms which it necessitated was expensive, and in complex patterns its use required great technical skill. Each Jacquard 'card' carried a portion of the design, and all had to be accurately coordinated in conjunction with the warp threads during the weaving. In 1836-8 the Jacquard system was used to make imitation Chantilly, the pattern being woven by machine and the cordonnet run in by hand. In 1841 a modification was invented which enabled the machine to make the cordonnet itself. The Great Exhibition of 1851, with enormous prizes offered by Prince Albert, and the International Exhibition of 1867 were great stimulants to machine design and manufacture.

The overall effect was fourfold:

1. Handmade lace was no longer a status symbol, the machine imitations being so painstakingly accurate that they could only with difficulty be distinguished from the real thing.
2. Lace was therefore no longer exclusive. Machine lace, as its production multiplied, became quite cheap and within the reach of almost everyone.
3. Although lace was now as a consequence extremely popular, it was no longer possible for handmade lace of any real fineness to be produced economically. Only special orders for the rich or royal could finance the many hands and many hours of work needed to produce a garment of quality. In 1840 it had been difficult to find enough Honiton

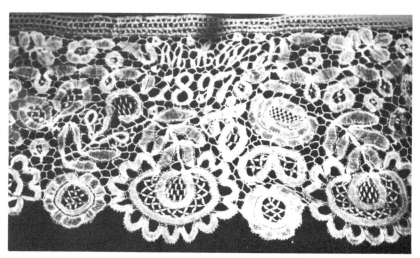

8. Honiton bobbin lace dated 1897. (170 mm.)

9 (below left). Messina crochet. The label reads: 'Bought from the Ragged School in the new town outside Messina, 1912. Handmade. After the earthquake which destroyed Messina.' See Provenance, page 24. (Length of lace shown: 41 mm.)
10 (below right). Needlerun net with machine picot. The label reads: 'Brussels lace made by Madame Schellekens de Pauw (Belgian refugee from Lierre) November 1915 in Bromley — Kent'. (82 mm.)

workers to make Queen Victoria's £1,000 wedding gown, 'a white satin gown, with a very deep flounce of Honiton lace, an imitation of an old design'.✱ In 1841, by royal patronage, the Honiton workers made 'a white Honiton point lace robe and mantle, over white satin'✱ for the christening of Victoria's firstborn, the Princess Royal. This same robe and mantle were used at the christening of all Victoria's nine children, while the Queen herself on these occasions wore her bridal flounce transferred from one dress to another. Superb Honiton was also made for the wedding gowns of Queen Alexandra in 1863 and of Queen Mary in 1893. A photograph of Queen Victoria, taken in the Jubilee year of 1887, shows her wearing an apron and small veil of elaborate Honiton guipure, which may or may not have represented some residue of her bridal lace.

4. The more quickly a lace could be made, the more commercially viable it was, and thus Irish crochet, knitted lace, embroidered net, filet and tape laces prospered at the expense of the more beautiful but more laborious bobbin and needlepoint laces.

In the 1880s came the invention of chemical lace in Switzerland and Germany. This was a derivative of machine embroidery whereby the background material, which was usually silk, was dissolved or corroded away by chlorine or caustic soda, leaving only the cotton embroidery itself. Designs were ingenious and could appear from a short distance strikingly similar to reticella, punto in aria, Venetian Point, Irish crochet, Honiton or Brussels.

The relative popularity of lace as ornament continued into the twentieth century and some fine-quality Brussels lace, in particular Point de Gaz, and some English and French laces were produced for the Edwardian rich and their children. However, from the 1920s lace went into a decline from which it is only just beginning to recover. Until the late 1960s only a few sought for and preserved the old laces; only a very few schools or classes existed for the teaching of lacemaking; and it was only in the 1970s that lace as a garniture of dress came back into fashion. Let us hope that by the efforts of the new lacemakers the art of twisting thread into beautiful patterns may be preserved for ever.

✱ Quotations from Queen Victoria's journal, 10th February, 1840 (the day of her wedding) and 10th February, 1841.

A NOTE ON TERMINOLOGY

Lace is in itself a complex subject and it is therefore all the more unfortunate that its study is further complicated by the use of foreign terms, of alternative terms, and by contradictory usage.

Foreign terms

These take the form of a hotchpotch of French and Italian, sometimes anglicised in pronunciation and sometimes not, sometimes with English equivalents and sometimes not. Examples are: *reseau* for the handmade mesh; *Point d'Angleterre* for a form of eighteenth-century Flemish lace; *Gros Point, Point de Neige* and *Reseau Venise* for three forms of Venetian needlepoint; *reticella* and *punto in aria* for early Italian needlepoints. The terms *punto tirato* and *punto tagliato* have been largely replaced by 'drawn and pulled threadwork' and 'cutwork'.

Alternative terms

For example, mesh, net, ground, fond and reseau are used as equivalents; so are brides, bars and bridges; also point d'esprit, spots, dots, leadworks, plaits and tallies; and Point de Paris reseau, six-point star, fond chant, French ground, wire ground and Kat stitch. In the text I have used 'net' solely for a machine-made product. If the term is allowed to extend to handmade laces, as it does for example in Honiton net stitch and Bucks net ground, then the terms 'bobbin net' and 'Brussels net', used of the products of the twist net machines since they were first invented, become incomprehensible.

Contradictory usage

One striking example is in the use of the simple terms 'footing' and 'heading', which in an edging refer normally to the straight border which will be attached to the material it is decorating, and to the free border. However both Mrs Palliser and Jourdain, in their glossaries, make them synonymous.

Although in all the books on the history of lace the term 'needlepoint' has a perfectly clear meaning of laces built up from buttonhole stitches, 'needlepoint' in American everyday use means embroidery, and a suggestion has been made that in reference to lace the term 'needle' rather than 'needlepoint' should be used.

'Drawn threadwork' and 'pulled threadwork' are slightly confusing terms — in much the same way as when one is told that the curtains have been drawn a slight doubt may arise as to whether they have been drawn across or back. Traditionally, in drawn threadwork the warp or weft threads are *drawn out* and removed, while in pulled threadwork they are not removed but are *pulled together*. A recent suggestion has been made that the terms 'drawn thread' and 'drawn fabric' (for drawn and pulled thread) might be less open to misinterpretation.

Though many books on lace use the feminine ending 'reticella', the masculine 'reticello' as in Ricci's book is more correct.

The naming of laces is at variance between collectors, countries and continents. This may be because the donation of lace collections to museums does not antedate the second half of the nineteenth century and detailed comparative research of these collections is still incomplete. The discrepancies of identification between one book on the history of lace and another must have been glaringly obvious since they were first published between fifty and one hundred years ago, but now that comparisons can be made and local provenances discussed it should be possible for a generally agreed usage of lace terms and titles to be laid down. At the time when Mrs Palliser's collection of samples was donated to Exeter Museum in 1869 she had had to be largely independent in her attributions and nomenclature, having no other extensive collection to refer to. The originality of some of her identifications is now rather irritating, and it might appear that many of her examples were named simply from the places where she bought them.

I will give just one example of the contradictory usage of lace names which must exasperate the expert as well as confuse the beginner. 'Point lace' is a highly ambiguous term. Derived, it is to be supposed, from the French *point* meaning stitch, it is commonly used as an abbreviation for needlepoint lace, as in Gros Point and Hollie Point. However, it is also commonly used of any fine-quality lace whether made by bobbins or buttonhole stitching, as in Honiton Point, Bucks Point and Point d'Angleterre. Again it was used of the late nineteenth-century tape lace imitations of early Italian laces, as in Daisy Waterhouse Hawkins's *Old Point Lace and How to Copy It*, published in 1878. I have even heard point lace defined as any lace which has a dentate (toothed, i.e. pointed) edge. Point ground and point net are other names used for fond simple; and point net is also the name of a net produced in the late eighteenth century on the Stocking Frame machine. Point de Paris is used both of a reseau and of a type of Normandy lace which has this reseau.

To go into any more detail of these disparate terms would be to overweight this small book with argument. I therefore refer the reader to the glossary for the definitions which I have chosen to use in the text, as being, I believe, those in most common acceptance by the majority of lacemakers and lace collectors.

IDENTIFYING LACE

One could very broadly divide the main types of laces by the centuries in which they were at their peak:

sixteenth century — embroidered laces;
seventeenth century — needlepoint laces;
eighteenth century — bobbin laces;
nineteenth century — machine laces, embroidered nets and other 'imitation' laces.

In identifying a piece of lace one needs to be able to pinpoint four things:

1. Which of the main types, above, it belongs to, that is the type of technique employed;
2. Which subdivision within that type;
3. The country of origin;
4. The age.

The subdivision and the country of origin may well be the same. Many laces are named after the country, county, city, town or village where they originated, or with which they have been in the past mainly associated. However, as any present-day lacemaker knows, Buckingham and Bedfordshire laces may be made in Devon or indeed, as they have been during the twentieth century, in India, China, or wherever missionary zeal in the convent schools may have carried them. Thus while the subdivision of type may be fairly accurately determined, the country of origin even of sixteenth- and seventeenth-century laces must often have a question mark accompanying it.

The age, too, is difficult. There are certain date lines, for example:

(a) The gossamer-fine flax thread of northern Europe did not survive past 1800, and therefore lace made of this thread cannot be later than the end of the eighteenth century.

(b) Machine net in its usual form was not invented until the early nineteenth century, and so cannot be earlier than that.

(c) Cotton. It was not until about 1833 that a cotton thread was produced strong enough to be used for handmade lace, therefore handmade cotton laces are later than 1833.

(d) Linen. On the other hand, linens of the sixteenth-century type, handspun and handwoven, were made throughout the last four hundred years up to the 1930s, mainly in the peasant regions of north

Italy and central Europe, so that identification of these by age is often hard. All one can say is that commercial handwoven linens, used for example for cutwork or drawn threadwork, must be earlier than 1930. Conversely, machine-woven linens, identifiable by the regularity of the weave, will be later than 1785, when Cartwright's steam power loom was invented.

(e) Design. Another difficulty in dating is that it was common practice for early eighteenth-century needlepoints to be made to seventeenth-century designs. Indeed one of the contributing factors to the decline of the Venetian lace industry was that it failed to adapt to the eighteenth-century fashions and the types of lace which they required. Then again, in the various revivals attempted during the nineteenth century, copies were made of earlier laces, for example of Venetian and Alençon at Burano, and it is by no means easy to say whether a piece of Venetian Gros Point which does not look or feel 'right' is a piece of bad seventeenth-century workmanship or a nineteenth-century imitation. As late as the 1920s the Amelia Ars Society of Bologna was making brilliant copies of Vinciolo's designs for punto in aria, but the pieces which they produced are rare and must be regarded as works of art rather than as commercial substitutes. Even nowadays, if an old parchment of Buckingham lace, for example, is used and the design and technique accurately copied, it may be almost impossible after the passage of only two or three years to be able to date this new production precisely simply by looking at it.

(f) Portraits and paintings, for example of lace workers by named artists, give important indications of the *type* of lace in use, or being made, during that period. One such portrait obviously would not be conclusive — it could be somebody in fancy dress — but repetitions would provide cumulative and eventually conclusive evidence.

(g) Provenance. One difficulty in the precise dating of any *particular piece* of lace is that, unlike many other antiques, it bears no factory mark, maker's mark or signature. In the rare instances where dates are found worked into the lace the probability of this being the actual year when the lace was made is very high, though the possibility that it is a commemorative date referring to some earlier event cannot be ruled out. Pieces of paper pinned or stitched to lace are interesting but not infallible indications. It is common in old boxes of lace to find loose labels, and these can be attached in good faith to quite the wrong pieces. Documentation of family lace similarly may not apply to the piece to which it is now said to refer. Innocent substitutions can all too easily occur when lace passes by inheritance or purchase from one owner to another or is disturbed simply by a change of residence. Nor can one completely overlook the intention to deceive in this question of age or identity. However, with regard to modern 'forgeries', lace has the advantage that it can scarcely now be produced in less time or with less expense than it could several hundred years ago, and therefore, since old lace is currently vastly undervalued and in many cases changes hands at a cost less than the Stuart kings paid for it, the faker must be financially out of pocket and so defeat his own purpose. A Bucks handkerchief edging for example, made in 1977 to a nineteenth-century design, was priced by the maker at £100, while an actual nineteenth-century edging would probably then have fetched less than £5 even in a specialist saleroom.

I shall now consider in detail the four main types of lace and how to distinguish them from each other.

1. Embroidered laces

(a) CUTWORK

Cutwork, in the sixteenth century, was made both in northern and southern Europe. It is easy to identify, for it consisted only of holes cut in the linen and then embroidered around, usually in white thread. Sometimes the holes were crossed by bars or partially filled with needlepoint designs. The linen was handspun and handwoven. Its handspun nature is identifiable by the frequent joins in the thread since only short lengths could be spun at a time and each join was marked by a slight lumpiness. Before the mid sixteenth century only a distaff existed, but then a form of spinning wheel with the wheel turned by a foot treadle, so that it left both hands free, was invented. No further mechanisation occurred until the second half of the eighteenth century, when Hargreaves in 1764 invented the Spinning Jenny. Therefore only after this date could greater lengths be smoothly spun so that the frequent irregularities of the thread disappeared. The early cutwork linen was of a cold, heavy texture, but supple and with a fine feel to it. As a result of wear over many years the threads under a magnifier are likely to be quite smooth and lacking in fluffiness. Fluffiness is not, however, an infallible criterion — some pieces known to have been made not later than 1700 may exhibit it, from having been put carefully away, unused, perhaps for some sad reason. I have seen, for example, a complete seventeenth-century baby's set of long bib, cuffs, bonnet and mittens, edged with lace, and looking as fluffy and new as if it had been made yesterday. Thus fluffy thread indicating lack of wear may or may not indicate also a recent origin and, if the design too is the same, accurate dating becomes almost impossible. Later cutwork often did, however, show contemporary in-

11. Sixteenth-century cutwork, part of a coverlet. Note the simple oversewing stitches around the cut holes, and the bars worked over with buttonhole stitch. (230 mm.)

fluence at work in its designs. Also, though in country areas the linen continued to be handwoven, especially for use by embroiderers, from the late eighteenth century much was machine-woven.

Cutwork derivatives are the Madeira or Chinese tablecloths of late nineteenth- or early twentieth-century origin. In these the linen is usually machine-woven and the decoration of an art nouveau or deco type.

Another derivative was broderie anglaise, popular through the second half of the nineteenth century into Edwardian times (page 148).

Some excellent cutwork was produced by the Ruskin Craft Centre at Coniston in the Lake District in the late nineteenth century (page 28).

(b) DRAWN AND PULLED THREADWORK

In technique the early form in no way differs from any work of the kind made subsequently, even up to the present day. It was worked on hand-spun and handwoven linen, and the silk embroidery threads used might be white, red or black. Some has survived from fifteenth-century Russia. In

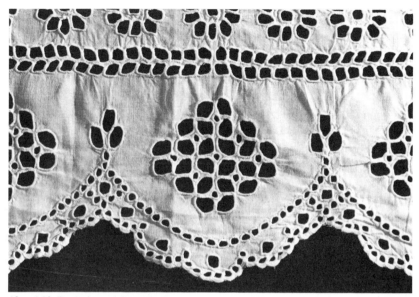

12 and 13. Broderie anglaise, mid nineteenth century (above), and Madeira work, twentieth century (below). The technique is the same as in 11, but the designs are typical of their period. (Broderie anglaise 180 mm; Madeira work 360 mm.)

drawn threadwork some of the threads are removed; in pulled work they are pulled together and bound round with stitching so that both outline and detail are indicated by small holes. The early designs were of angels, monsters, sacred animals and trees. Because of the right-angular arrangement of the warp and weft they were sharply cornered and boxy-looking.

One of the main derivatives of this type of lace was the Dresden work, sometimes inaccurately called Tönder work, produced in Denmark and north Germany in the late seventeenth and eighteenth centuries. It was very popular and exports from Denmark to Germany and the Baltic in the mid eighteenth century are said to have exceeded £11,000. At first its designs were fairly heavy, like the sixteenth-century work, though the arrangements of threads and types of stitches were infinitely more varied. In the second half of the eighteenth century, in line with the misty wispy nature of the bobbin laces then in fashion, the linen used was of exceptional lightness and fineness. In the last decade of the century a translucent cotton muslin from India replaced the linen. The work was punto tirato at its supreme excellence: it surpasses belief that thread, needle, patience and eyesight could have been so acute and so unerring in the counting of the minute threads of the material and in the faultless linking of them into superb and delicate designs.

In the early nineteenth century this type of work was deteriorating on the continent, but it was carried on in the United Kingdom in a modified and diminished form known as Ayrshire work (page 144).

It was also the subject of one of the craft revivals in nineteenth-century England, instigated by the writer and artist John Ruskin (1819-1900). When he settled near Coniston in the Lake District in the early 1870s he had several spinning wheels made to an old design and encouraged the country folk to spin thread from flax imported from Belgium. This gave them a small income, as well as perhaps satisfying in Ruskin himself a somewhat puritanical need to occupy 'idle hands'. Subsequently he brought back designs of so-called Greek lace from Italy, and the hand-spun linen was decorated with cutwork, drawnwork, reticella and needle-weaving. As with most revival work, even that which carefully copied old designs, a certain stiffness of appearance distinguishes it from the verve and spontaneity of the 300-400 year old originals. Ruskin lace also possessed a number of technically distinctive features such as a typical drawn thread border to each cut-out panel. A certain amount of this work is still produced in the Flax Home Industry at Grasmere, the only one surviving of the eight which existed in Ruskin's time. An evenweave machine linen of twenty-eight threads to the inch is now used, and for the embroidery or needlepoint a slightly thicker flax thread.

Some very similar work was produced by the Sioux Indians of North

14. Pulled threadwork, a typical sixteenth-century design, though a later copy. Note the sharp angles of the winged figures repelling the dragons. (250 mm.)

15. The technique of drawn threadwork. The basic linen is shown at the lower border. Some of the threads above have been removed and the rest bound tightly around to produce the square-meshed ground. The pattern appears where pieces of the linen have been left intact. Part of a sixteenth-century altar cloth. (50 mm.)

16. Dresden work, part of the border of a fichu, mid eighteenth century. The very fine basic material is shown above. To produce the elaborate patterning below, these threads have been counted and pulled evenly together in an amazing variety of designs, some twelve different ones being shown in this 200 mm length.

17. Baltic pulled threadwork, the solid parts strengthened with shadow stitch, showing a pelican piercing its breast with its beak to feed its young with its blood. Second half of the eighteenth century. (300 mm.)

18. Ayrshire work, detail from the embroidered skirt panel of a christening gown, c. 1840. The lower three petals of the central flower show drawn work, the upper four pulled work. The heart of the flower has been cut out and the hole filled with a design of buttonhole-stitched circles suspended from a needlepoint rim. As in Dresden work, the threads to be counted are very fine and the whole piece is only 80 mm across.

America in the late nineteenth century under the tutorship of Sybil Carter, and the Indian Lace Association was founded.

In the main, identification of this type of lace presents no problems — the threads can be *seen* to be pulled together or removed. However, some of the old punto tirato may appear superficially like two other forms of embroidered lace: filet or lacis, and Buratto.

19. Philippine drawn and pulled work on pina cloth; part of a handkerchief, nineteenth century. (320 mm.)

20. Filet, showing the hand-knotted ground stretched on a frame and the darning of a cupid in progress. Nineteenth century. (Width of metal frame 200 mm.)

(c) FILET AND BURATTO

Both of these date from early times. Filet consisted of a hand-knotted background, similar to a fisherman's net. The meshes were usually square, but occasionally diamond-shaped, especially in Spanish lace. On this background the design was embroidered, using a darning stitch. Variations in the thickness of the thread could produce a shaded effect.

In Buratto the background appeared similar, but it was woven, so that its production was speedier. It lacked the knotting so characteristic of filet.

Both these types were made continuously from the sixteenth century to the present day. Filet was particularly popular around 1900 as Italian tourist pieces. Tablecloths, coverlets and wall hangings made entirely of filet, or of filet insertions in cotton or linen material, have been produced in China in recent times.

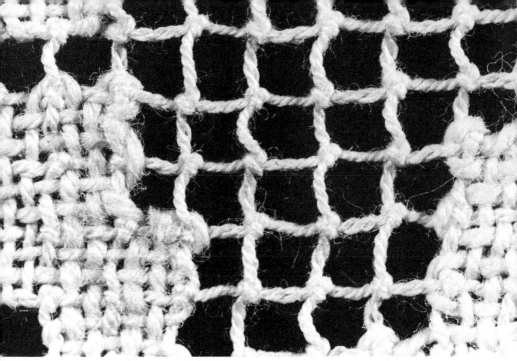

21. Filet: a close-up of the ground. The knotting can be clearly seen, and also the course of the threads darned in and out of the mesh. (16 mm.)

22. Buratto. Unlike filet, the ground is woven, in this very typical manner, and there is no knotting. (16 mm.)

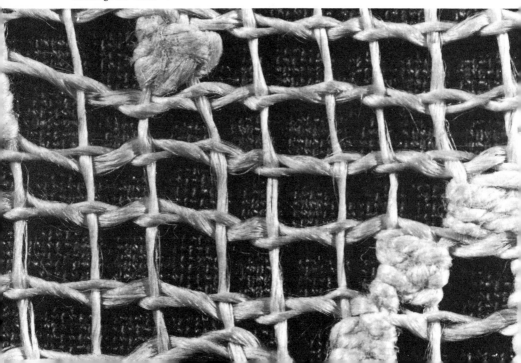

23. Buratto, part of a sixteenth-century altar border. As in filet, the design is darned on the ground and is necessarily angular. (180 mm.)

24. Reticella, part of a sampler, c. 1600. The typical square skeletons of linen are visible, forming the frame for the needlepoint designs. In many, though not all, diagonals have been stretched across the frames. (190 mm.)

2. Needlepoint laces

The fundamental unit of all needlepoints is buttonhole stitch, and it is of course made with a needle. Thus while the basic appearance of bobbin lace resembles weaving, or occasionally plaiting, the basic appearance of needlepoint resembles embroidery, and this is the first thing to look for.

The earliest needlepoints are (a) reticella and (b) punto in aria. Both are characterised by a geometric design made up of squares and circles.

(a) RETICELLA

As was explained earlier, reticella was basically a filling in of a hole made in the linen material by the extensive removal of threads to form a frame between a half and three inches (13-75 millimetres) square. Within this frame the space was first traversed by diagonals and then filled to a greater or lesser extent by row upon row of closely worked buttonhole stitches to form a solid-looking, evenly textured design of which fifty or more variations were possible. It was therefore, of necessity, a kind of

25. Reticella insertion, early seventeenth century, showing an attempt to break away from purely geometric forms. In the centre are two people on horseback on either side of a central tower, and above and below strange animals and birds. (240 mm.)

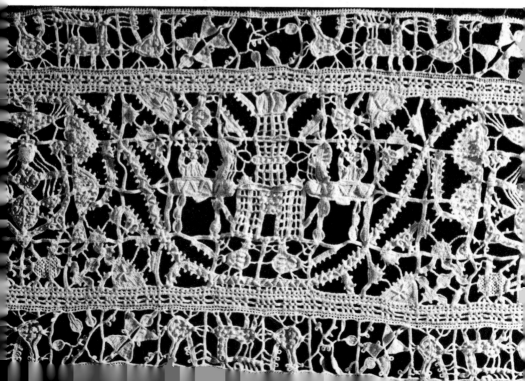

insertion. It can be recognised by the square frame of its units, by the diagonals and by the stitch itself, which is visible with a magnifier.

(b) PUNTO IN ARIA

Punto in aria, on the other hand, was primarily an edging, lacking in its making any connection with the material it was intended to decorate. It had a dentate edge, more or less sharply pointed, such as one sees on ruffs and cuffs in portraits of the sixteenth and seventeenth centuries. It can be identified by the buttonhole stitching, but it could at a casual glance be confused with some forms of Genoese bobbin lace which set out quite deliberately to imitate it, using a plaiting or knotting technique.

26. Punto in aria: part of a handkerchief border, late sixteenth century. There is no vestige of linen in the border, which is made entirely by the twisting of threads in buttonhole stitches. A maned lion with a tiny beaded eye is visible to the right, and hounds and turkeys in the inset panel. (160 mm.)

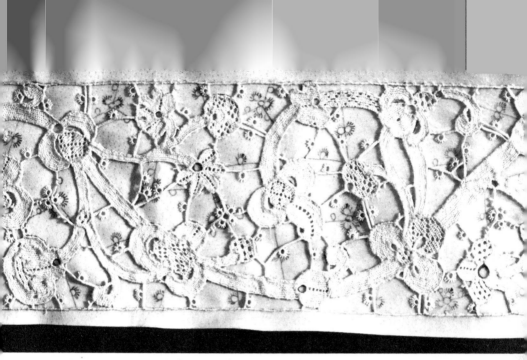

27. The making of a needlepoint lace. The pattern is drawn on a strip of parchment, outlining threads are tacked down along the edges of the design, and the spaces between them are filled with buttonhole stitches. When this work is complete the linking brides are put in to hold the toilé together. Finally the tacking threads are cut, and the lace is removed from the parchment, which can then be used again. (180 mm.)

(c) HOLLIE POINT

This is generally regarded as an English lace and it is placed here because of the geometric appearance of the design and because of the technique, which differed markedly from that of the other needlepoints. It was a very flat lace made in a continuous strip rather like a tape. Neat straight rows of tiny buttonhole stitches were worked from one side of the strip to the other, and the design was formed by a regular spacing of the stitches so that gaps were left like small pinholes, and eventually the Lamb of God, the Holy Dove, the Lily of the Annunciation or the Tree of Knowledge with Adam and Eve would appear in outline and detail like a pinwork picture. It was used mainly in christening sets, along the crown of the baby's linen cap and the shoulders of his shirt, on his mittens and cuffs. It is recorded in the sixteenth, seventeenth and eighteenth centuries, but most of the dated examples are from the second half of the eighteenth century, or even the early nineteenth century, at which time the work was somewhat coarser and looser.

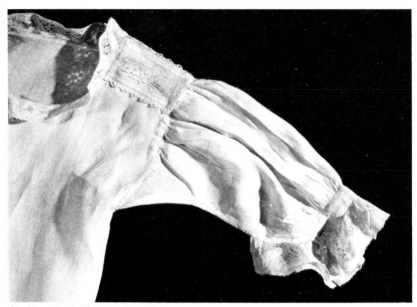

28. Part of a baby's shirt, early eighteenth century, showing a Hollie Point panel on the shoulder. The gusset and sleeve seams also have a thin insertion of Hollie Point. The neck and wrists are edged with Mechlin lace. (240 mm to end of cuff.)

29. The Hollie Point panel of the Lamb of God enlarged. Note the even parallel rows of buttonhole stitching which make the solid ground, the outline and detail of the design being formed by spaced stitches leaving small holes. (80 mm.)

All the remaining needlepoints, from whatever country of origin, were non-geometric and were made in the same general way, that is the motifs — whether flowers, people or animals — were worked as separate units, then arranged in accordance with the design and finally linked by brides of various kinds or by a reseau.

(d) VENETIAN NEEDLEPOINTS

Six distinct types were made from the early seventeenth century to the mid eighteenth. Of these (i) Gros Point, (ii) Rose Point and (iii) Point de Neige consisted of elaborately raised floral or leafy encrustments of diminishing size from (i) to (iii).

i. Gros Point

The Gros Point motifs might be more than 2 inches (50 millimetres) across, with a wide cordonnet padded with wool, and linked by short brides decorated with picots.

ii. Rose Point

In Rose Point the flowers were smaller and the cordonnet less raised, but the flowers were tiered and the brides more elaborate. Although in

30. Gros Point, first half of the seventeenth century. The large flowers measure between 50 and 75 mm across. The flax thread is exceptionally fine with a silky gloss, the stitches almost invisible except with a good magnifier. Note the padded cordonnet, spiked with picots, and the broad decorative brides. (340 mm.)

31. Rose Point, mid seventeenth century. The frequency of the 'knobbly caterpillar' may indicate a Spanish origin. The flowers are smaller, 25-40 mm across. (200 mm.)

32. Point de Neige, second half of the seventeenth century. The small size of the motifs, about 13 mm across, the elaborately built-up picots of the cordonnet and the decorated brides are typical. (90 mm.)

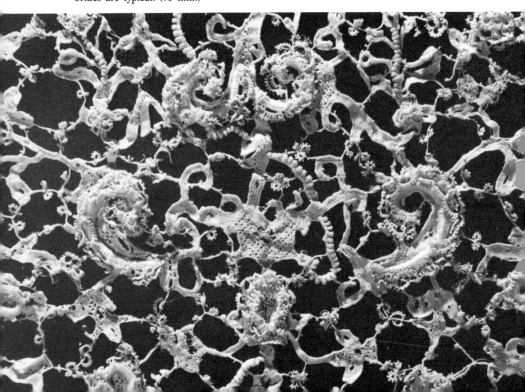

their extreme forms Gros Point and Rose Point seem quite distinct, there are many intermediate examples, and some authors do not separate them. In fact they regard 'rose' as a corruption of 'raised'.

iii. Point de Neige

This trend, towards flowers which were smaller but built up in delicate layers, and towards increasingly decorative brides, reached its peak in Point de Neige. Once seen, none of these three can be confused with any other lace, except perhaps similar and contemporary forms from Spain, and a few later copies.

The remaining three types were flat, as opposed to raised, laces.

iv. Point Plat

Point Plat was a beautiful closely worked lace, following the general scrolling design of the raised points, but the flowers instead of being padded and tiered were embellished with a wonderfully imaginative multitude of fillings producing a very pretty effect. It was largely used for edging the fashionable linen aprons of that day and for alb flounces.

33. Point Plat. There is no cordonnet, the toilé is quite flat, the design delicately varied, and the brides starred with picots. (200 mm.)

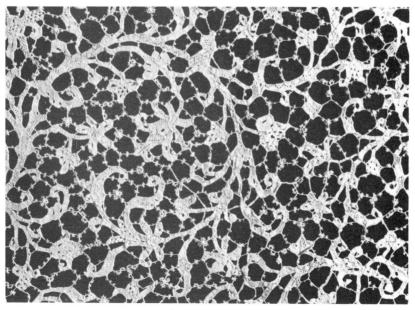

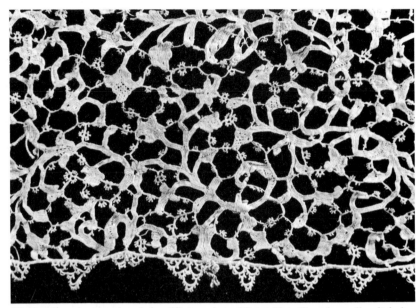

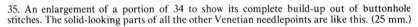

34. Coralline. A reduced and simplified version of Point Plat. Though smaller, it is less delicate in appearance. (100 mm.)

35. An enlargement of a portion of 34 to show its complete build-up out of buttonhole stitches. The solid-looking parts of all the other Venetian needlepoints are like this. (25 mm.)

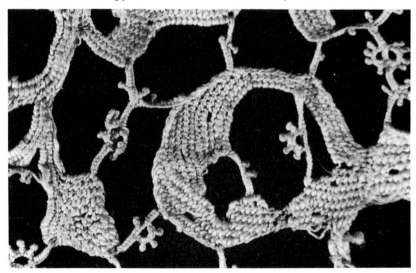

36. Reseau Venise, again completely flat. The chevrons in the design are typical, the reseau of the Alençon type, the whole texture gossamer fine. (120 mm.)

v. Coralline

This term is used to refer to a rather degenerate form of Point Plat, where the design has been largely lost and the fillings are limited in type. There was no cordonnet, but occasionally there was a slight raising of the motifs, which may have been a later addition.

vi. Reseau- Venise

This was a flat needlepoint of extremely fine texture, with an elaborate and beautiful design of formalised lilies, filled with a multitude of fantastic ornament, of which the zigzag or chevron was particularly characteristic. It is a rare lace, and its date of origin is uncertain — late seventeenth century according to some authorities, but on the whole the first half of the eighteenth century seems more likely, when it might have developed as a rival to the cobweb-like bobbin laces so popular then. It had a fragile looped reseau similar to that of the French Alençon needlepoint which had begun in the early eighteenth century. Indeed its place of origin has been disputed, and while there is no doubt whatever that lace of this distinctive type exists, only further research can determine exactly from where and when it came.

vii. Tape lace

Tape lace of a kind was made during the seventeenth century in Italy. It used a woven or bobbin tape of even width, folded rather clumsily and not at all neatly fixed, to form the outline of a Gros Point or Rose Point design, which was then filled in with buttonhole stitch.

viii. Renaissance lace

A derivative of this seventeenth-century tape lace was the so-called Renaissance (rebirth) lace. This was a deliberate attempt to revive old designs by copying the Italian tape laces which themselves had imitated in an abbreviated manner the entirely needlepoint Venetian laces. The classic book on this type of work was Daisy Waterhouse Hawkins's *Old Point Lace and How to Copy It* published in 1878. Her introductory chapter makes it clear that the aim, constantly recurring throughout the nineteenth century, was a rebellion against mechanisation and the products of 'the iron wheels set a-going by steam'. She says: 'The aim of making lace by hand is to revive the ancient art . . . So far as the materials employed, and the delicacy and variety of stitches, the same degree of perfection has been already attained by our modern workers as by their ancient predecessors . . . but there is still one most important portion of the work which continues to be comparatively neglected, and that is, the design, in consequence of which neglect, modern point lace is, when compared with old lace, like a body without a soul. The want of variety and beauty in design is the more remarkable since the work is chiefly undertaken by the most refined enjoyers of "elegant leisure", who are supposed to possess an amount of delicate fancy and taste, scarcely to be expected from those who "stitch, stitch, stitch" merely to keep themselves alive on bread and tea. The difference between the patterns now used for point lace and the old specimens is this,— the modern lace consists of an exact and continuous repetition of a design, which is contained in four or five inches of space, whereas the old lace displays a constant variety and change in the pattern throughout the entire length of the piece . . . in this consists the superiority of *hand* over *machine* made lace.'

ix. Burano

Burano, an island near Venice, was a centre for lace production during the eighteenth century, but this industry had died out by 1866, and little of the eighteenth-century lace survives except in museums. It was revived in 1872 when the fishing industry failed and the people were in danger of starvation. From that time until the end of the century imitations of the early Venetian needlepoints, and also of the eighteenth-century French, were produced. These can provide a trap for the collector, since the copies

plication here is that some eighteenth-century Alençon, or Argentan, was during the nineteenth century regrounded in Burano — presumably because the original reseau had gone into holes — thus you may find a combination of Alençon motifs, with their typical cordonnet, and an equally typical Burano reseau.

(e) SPANISH NEEDLEPOINTS

The exact dating of these is difficult. They appear to have been contemporary with the Venetian laces and of almost identical design, though whether this was a case of mimicry or of parallel evolution it is impossible to say. A perusal of Florence May's book *Hispanic Lace and Lace Making* could make one believe that all the types of lace in the entire world emanated from Spain, but only one small point of design, which can best be described as a knobbly caterpillar, appears distinctively characteristic, apart from the two-headed imperial eagle, which, being part of the Spanish royal arms, does not appear in Venetian laces — unless any lace for the king of Spain or his family was especially ordered from Venice. But Spain did not have the monopoly of this symbol. The two-headed eagle had appeared in the arms of the German-Roman empire from early times, and it was later chosen to represent Russian imperialism. But Spain was the only lacemaking country of the seventeenth and eighteenth centuries which had the right to use it.

(f) FRENCH NEEDLEPOINTS

These at least are known to have followed the Venetian needlepoints.

i. Point de France

By about 1660, during the reign of Louis XIV (1643-1715), the sums of money spent by the French court on Venetian laces had become so immense that a series of sumptuary edicts was passed prohibiting the importation of foreign laces. They were, however, even less effective than the acts of Parliament of Charles I and II of England. The native French laces of that time were of poor quality and unpopular. Colbert, then secretary to the statesman Mazarin, initiated the development of a new lace centre at Alençon in Normandy in 1665. The superb needlepoint produced there won the approval of the king, who gave it the name Point de France. It was adopted by court etiquette, and the wearing of it became compulsory. It continued to be used in the greatest profusion throughout Louis XIV's reign, not only on clothing but also decorating towels, baths and dressing tables. Its later design, though rich and picturesque, was a kind of subdued rococo, in contrast to the baroque extravagance of the Venetian laces. The motifs were relatively small, with only a slightly raised cordonnet, but its most distinctive feature was the ground of brides picotées

40. Point de France: part of a collar, late seventeenth century. Note the voluptuous design, the rather insignificant cordonnet, and the ground of brides picotées arranged in hexagons. (200 mm.)

41. Argentella: part of a pair of lappets, early eighteenth century. The floral design is similar to point de France but lighter and more delicate; there is a more consistent cordonnet, and the ground is of a filled hexagon within a skeletal hexagon. (100 mm.)

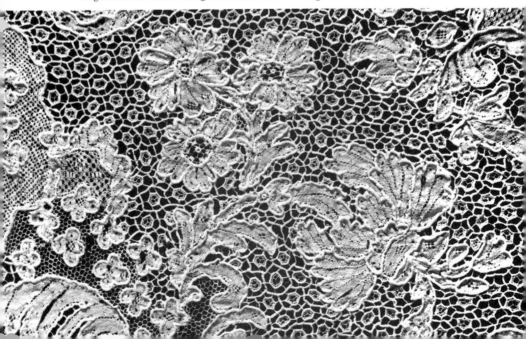

arranged in a series of hexagons. It was a heavy lace, and in the later seventeenth and early eighteenth centuries it gave rise to, and was eventually replaced by, three more lightweight needlepoints.

ii. Argentella

Argentella was characterised by an almost complete absence of brides or reseau, the spaces between the main floral design being filled with large and elaborate honeycombs made up of a solid hexagon within a skeletal hexagon. This lace is very rare, and some authorities regard it as a form of Argentan rather than as a distinctly separate form of lace.

iii. Argentan

The design was usually of scrolls or ribands, interspersed with flowers of a formal or semi-classical nature. There was a shallow cordonnet, and the reseau appeared of fairly large mesh. Every side of this mesh was worked closely over with buttonhole stitch, and though it may need a magnifying glass to distinguish this technique, it does not appear in any other lace and so is an important diagnostic characteristic. Argentan died out in the early nineteenth century. As with other needlepoint (and bobbin) laces, its early eighteenth-century form was almost entirely toilé, but later the design became simpler and the reseau more extensive, as a result of the need to speed production and to reduce its cost.

iv. Alençon

Alençon was scarcely distinguishable as a separate lace until in 1717 it developed a characteristic reseau consisting of looped stitches twisted around with thread. Another much quoted characteristic was the horsehair used to pad the stiffly raised cordonnet, covered firmly and unbrokenly with buttonhole stitching. Mrs Palliser, in a paragraph on Alençon where she says that it is the only lace using horsehair, refers to a lace made in Venice for Louis XIII (1601-43) in which the women workers used human hair because they could not find sufficiently fine horsehair. This lace was obviously not Alençon as it is now defined. Some authorities say that no horsehair was used after 1850, while others say it was not used until about 1850 and that it continues to be used today. Whatever the truth of nineteenth-century usage may be, fig. 52 shows horsehair enclosed by the picots around the cordonnet to provide support. The sharp ends of the hair tend to catch in the reseau and damage it. By the late eighteenth century Alençon had almost died out, but it was revived by Napoleon I, who on his marriage to Maria Louise of Austria in 1810 ordered Alençon bed curtains, tester, coverlet and pillow cases, all decorated with bees on a droschel ground. Production dwindled again, but during the Second Empire (1852-70) under Napoleon III some very fine

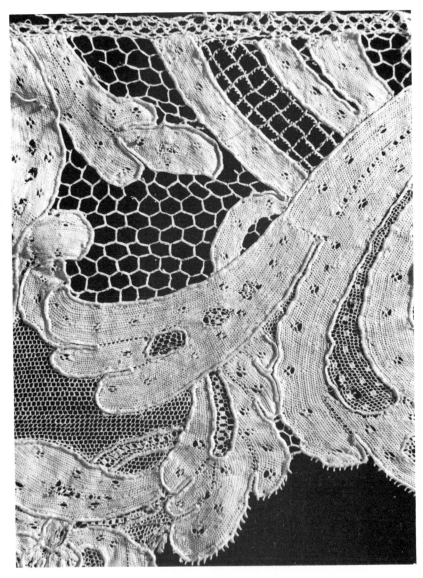

42. Argentan: part of a flounce, early eighteenth century. The design tends to be bolder and the mesh large sometimes to the point of clumsiness, but the workmanship is most painstaking, every side of the reseau being worked over with buttonhole stitching. As in 41 and 43 the cordonnet is closely oversewn with buttonhole stitches. Note the cut design at the top, indicating this was once a deeper flounce. (110 mm.)

43. Alençon, late eighteenth century. A more fragile lace than Argentan, the reseau not worked over with buttonhole stitching, but twisted around with thread in an attempt to strengthen it, though it is still easily broken especially by the sharp ends of horsehair which support the picots. (110 mm.)

pieces were made, one dress in 1855 being purchased by the Emperor for £2,800 as a gift for the Empress. Another dress, shown at the 1867 exhibition and priced at £3,400, had taken forty women seven years to complete. In the later eighteenth century Argentan and Alençon were used as winter laces and the bobbin laces of Mechlin, Lille, Caen and Spain as summer laces. Alençon is much more abundant than Argentan, since its simpler reseau made it quicker and cheaper to produce.

v. Point de Colbert

In the mid nineteenth century a lace manufacturer of Bayeux, Auguste Lefébure, who had already revived Alençon in 1855, made copies of some of the raised Venetian points. These were called Point de Colbert after the seventeenth-century minister who first founded the factories at Alençon. Fine as the workmanship was, the pieces had a hardness to them, perhaps to some extent the result of machine spinning as opposed to hand-

44. Point de Colbert, second half of the nineteenth century. Good workmanship, but the rigidity of design betrays its late origin. (200 mm.)
45. Netherlands needlepoint, seventeenth century. A rare piece, it shows a striking similarity in design to a Netherlands (Dutch) bobbin lace. (200 mm.)

46. Flemish needlepoint, eighteenth century, part of an engageant. A rare lace, distinguishable from Point de France, which the design to some extent resembles, by its greater fineness and by having a reseau instead of brides; and from reseau Venise, which it resembles in texture and dimensions, by the presence of a slightly raised cordonnet and the absence of chevrons. (90 mm.)

spinning, and the stitches were larger and the flax less silky than in the fabulous originals. They were less likely to be confused with those than were the slightly later Burano copies.

(g) ENGLISH NEEDLEPOINT

This seventeenth-century lace resembles more than anything fragments of Hollie Point of indeterminate shape linked together by plain or occasionally decorated brides. The toilé was flat, with no cordonnet, but of coarser thread than the Venetian Point Plat and with none of the swirling sprays of flowers and leaves which made that lace so prettily distinctive. Good examples are rare, but in these the small motifs were pricked into tiny patterns just as the strips of Hollie Point were, sometimes forming initials, a name or a date. At its worst English needlepoint was like a clumsy and enlarged Venetian Coralline. (See fig. 7.)

(h) BRUSSELS OR FLEMISH NEEDLEPOINT

Less needlepoint was made in Belgium or Flanders than in either Italy or France.

i. Flemish, eighteenth century

Flemish needlepoint, made in the eighteenth century, is as rare as reseau Venise, which it to some extent resembles. The two laces were similar in texture, but the Flemish was less strikingly ornamental and lacked the typical chevrons. It also had a very slightly raised cordonnet, while the reseau Venise was completely flat. It showed some continuity with the earlier and even rarer Dutch needlepoint.

ii. Point de Gaz

A derivative of Flemish needlepoint was the very well known Point de Gaz, one of the most delicate and expensive laces of the late nineteenth and early twentieth centuries. The thread was fine, the work of excellent design, close and firm. The toilé was characteristically of roses with tiers of petals, but there were also ribbon swathes and scrolls, candelabra and laburnum designs. The reseau was of needlemade loops, airily light and rather fragile, with no further thread twisted round as in Alençon, and no buttonholing over as in Argentan. The cordonnet was fixed by spaced buttonhole stitching. The designs of Point de Gaz and Alençon are usually so different that they cannot be confused, but some of the earlier pieces had a grandiose splendour which links them together. On the other hand, the Point de Gaz produced hurriedly and cheaply for the everyday market tended to be sparse of design, of loose texture, made of poor-quality cotton, and so to wear badly. Thus popularity led to a decline of quality, a fate which also overtook the English bobbin lace, Honiton.

47. Point de Gaz, late nineteenth century. The tiered rose petals, charming fillings, gauzy reseau and the cordonnet fixed by spaced buttonhole stitches are typical. (100 mm.) (See also fig. 60.)

iii. Brussels mixed

From about 1890 into the early twentieth century, medallions of Point de Gaz were occasionally incorporated into collars or flounces of Brussels bobbin lace, the result being called a 'mixed lace'.

(i) IRISH NEEDLEPOINT

Ireland, like Burano and Bayeux (Point de Colbert), played its part in producing quantities of bogus seventeenth-century Venetian raised point and flat point, and though some was very well done, the quality of the thread never approached the superlative fineness of the earlier work. Ireland also had a needlepoint lace which was entirely its own. It was begun in 1846 when the distress caused by the potato famine made some secondary occupation very needful. This lace is known as Youghal. The designs were mainly a bold flowing arrangement of wild flowers, the petals shaded by varying the closeness of the stitches to each other. The leaves were spiky in shape and the linking bars arranged in hexagons with numerous small picots, rather in the manner of Point de France, though on a bigger scale. The industry was supported by royalty: for example, Princess Maude of Wales ordered a fan of Youghal lace on the occasion of her marriage in 1896.

48. Youghal, second half of the nineteenth century, part of a collar. A pretty lace, with semi-naturalistic flowers, no raised cordonnet, a shaded effect produced by varying the distance apart of the buttonhole stitches, and a picoted ground superficially hexagonal but with curving sides. (230 mm.)

(j) TWENTIETH-CENTURY NEEDLEPOINTS

A kind of coarse needlepoint is still produced in various parts of the world, in particular Ireland, Belgium and Hong Kong, in the form of tablecloths and coverlets. Both material and design are stiff and lifeless and could in no way be mistaken for earlier laces. Although handmade, they lack identity and artistic spontaneity, and there are no distinctive differences between the products of one country and another.

Cyprus needlepoint is a nineteenth- and twentieth-century lace worked in buttonhole stitch to produce mainly tourist pieces, such as small mats, or geometric motifs for insertion into tablecloths. The thread is very rigid. It can be regarded as a derivative of 'Greek lace' or reticella.

49. Part of a needlepoint cloth from China, distinguished by a lack of all the good qualities of the earlier laces. A coarse cotton is used, the design is inartistic and the arrangement of brides untidy. (230 mm.)

50. Cyprus needlepoint of a tourist type, stiff and geometric. (80 mm.)

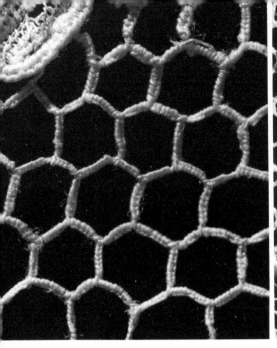

51 (above left). Argentan reseau: a large hexagonal mesh buttonholed over on all six sides. This also shows the close buttonhole stitching of the toilé and the tightly packed buttonholing of the cordonnet. Part of 42 enlarged. (12 mm.)

52 (above right). Alençon: the reseau mesh is smaller and is twisted around with thread, not buttonholed. The cordonnet is slightly padded, and horsehair supports the picots. (12 mm.)

53 (below left). Burano: the reseau is ladder-like, twisted around as in Alençon, the cordonnet loosely oversewn. (8 mm wide.)

54 (below right). Point de Gaz: the reseau is a simple loop like the basic Alençon, but with no additional twisting. The thread of the cordonnet is fixed by spaced buttonhole stitching. (8 mm wide.)

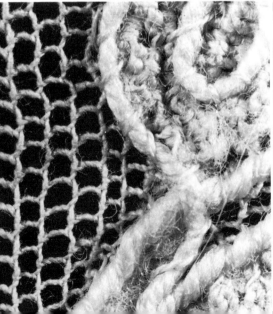
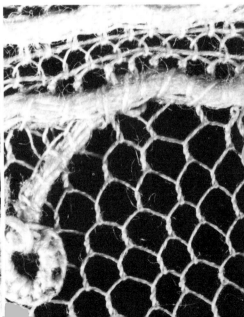

3. Bobbin laces

While bobbin laces were at their peak in the eighteenth century, bobbin-lace craftsmanship goes back certainly to the late sixteenth century, and a seventeenth-century portrait of a lacemaker by Steven van Duyven shows her using a pillow and bobbins similar to nineteenth-century ones.

Four criteria of identification have been discussed already with needlepoint laces: technique; design; material; reseau. Basically, the same generalisations hold true for bobbin laces.

Just as needlepoint laces have broadly a common *technique,* the use of buttonhole stitch, so have bobbin laces: the use of bobbins to pull the threads taut and facilitate handling while they are twisted, plaited or knotted, to form a more or less woven material. The design is first pricked, that is outlined by a series of pinholes, on parchment or stiff card. The pins which are stuck through these holes, into the pillow, hold and guide the threads as the lace is made. The number of bobbins required varies from about a dozen to several hundred depending on the width of the piece and the complexity of the design. The solid part of the design is referred to as the toilé, and the background is the mesh or reseau. One of the most obvious diagnostic features in distinguishing different kinds of bobbin lace is whether the toilé and reseau are worked as separate operations, as in Milanese, some Flemish, Brussels and Honiton, or whether they are worked together, as in all the others. This technique of working right across the lace from footing to heading is not used in needlepoint laces except in Hollie Point.

The *design* can be useful in dating, as well as in determining the place, or type, of origin. For example, up to the mid seventeenth century bobbin laces showed mainly geometrical forms with curves, triangles, diamonds and circles; for the next hundred years there were flowing lines, or-namental wreaths, garlands, stylised fruits and blossoms and scroll work. In the later eighteenth century the work became stilted and overcrowded until by 1800 the reseau was almost replacing the toilé, which was reduced to small sprigs, rosettes or simple insects. The only serious complications in this chronology resulted from the nineteenth-century practice of copying designs of the eighteenth or even seventeenth and sixteenth centuries. These copies can often be recognised as derivative, however, by an enlargement of the scale of the pattern caused by the use of a coarser thread. Designs of bobbin laces in the sixteenth, seventeenth and eighteenth centuries closely paralleled those of contemporary needlepoints in each country so that looking only at design it is possible to mistake, for example, Dutch needlepoint for the slightly commoner Dutch bobbin and the rare Venetian bobbin for Venetian Point Plat.

The *material* was almost entirely flax up to 1833, except for the gold

55. A pricking designed by Mr Tom Griffiths for the Jubilee gift from Honiton to Queen
Elizabeth II with dates 1952 and 1977, initials ER, and a spray of honeysuckle. 'Honiton'
was derived from 'Honey Town'. (150 mm.)

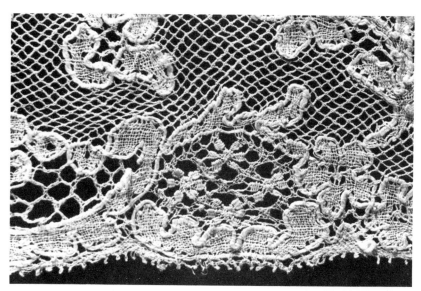

56. The technique of lace worked across in one piece. Note the continuity of thread between reseau and toilé and across the cordonnet into the picots. Note also the woven appearance of the toilé, which distinguishes it at once from the buttonhole-stitched toilé of needlepoint laces. (50 mm.)

57. The technique of toilé worked separately and then linked by reseau, or brides. Here the threads making the reseau carry across the back of the toilé so that the technique is easily identified. (50 mm.)

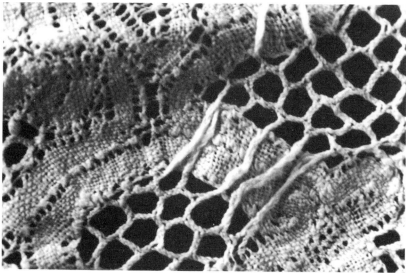

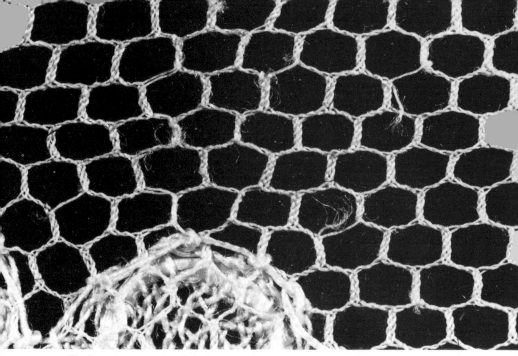

58. Brussels reseau/droschel. An approximately hexagonal mesh with two sides of four threads plaited four times and four sides of two threads twisted twice. This is the reverse side of the lace. At the foot of the figure is a piece of bobbin appliqué and the reseau can be seen continuing across the back of it; the attaching stitches, worked from this side, are clearly visible. Note the immense amount of work: this piece, as in figs. 59-67, measures only 13 mm across.

59. Mechlin: distinguished from droschel by having three plaits instead of four. This piece shows a tiny motif surrounded by a typical silky cordonnet and the continuity of thread between toilé and reseau indicating that the lace is worked right across. (13 mm.)

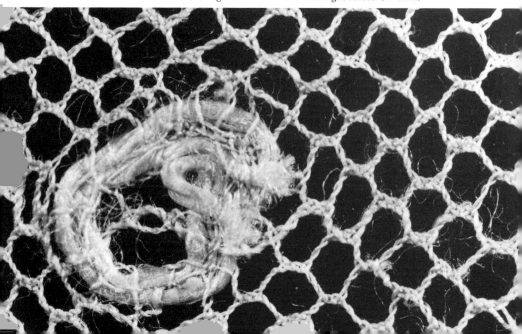

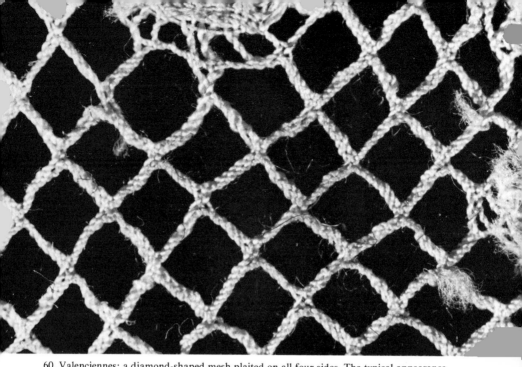

60. Valenciennes: a diamond-shaped mesh plaited on all four sides. The typical appearance of an outlining row of holes is shown at the top, and the continuity of thread between toilé and reseau is also visible. (13 mm.)

61. Round Valenciennes: plaited like Valenciennes on every side, but with a separation of the threads at the corners so that a hexagonal mesh is formed with a small hole at each angle. (13 mm.)

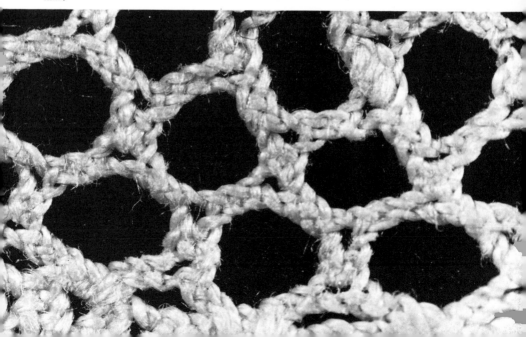

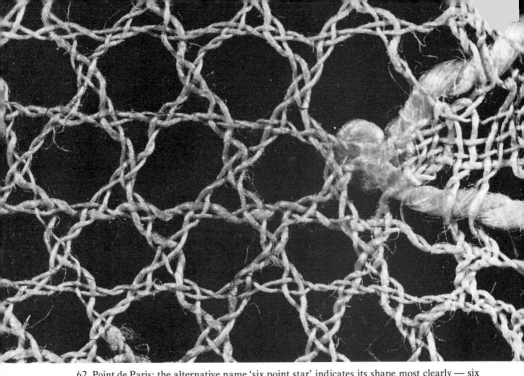

62. Point de Paris: the alternative name 'six point star' indicates its shape most clearly — six triangles around a central hexagon. The threads are twisted not plaited. (13 mm.)

63. Cinq trous (five holes): the square blocks of twisted thread outline four holes enclosing a central hole. (13 mm.)

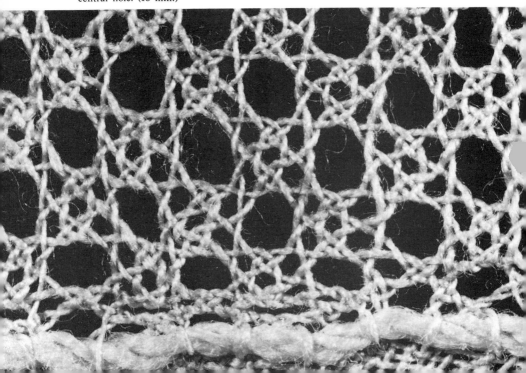

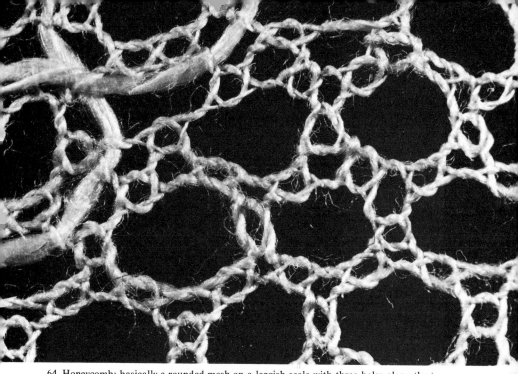

64. Honeycomb: basically a rounded mesh on a largish scale with three holes along the top and bottom and three on each side. (13 mm.)

65. Torchon: a diamond-shaped mesh, the interlacing of the twisted threads where they cross being very characteristic. (13 mm.)

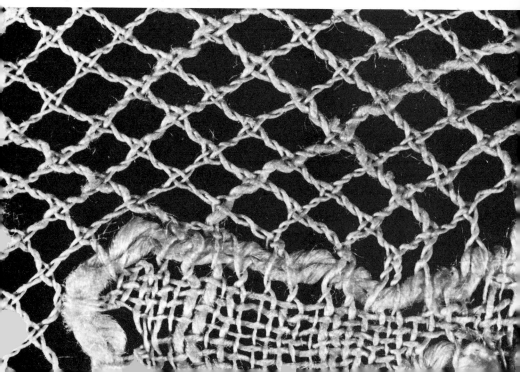

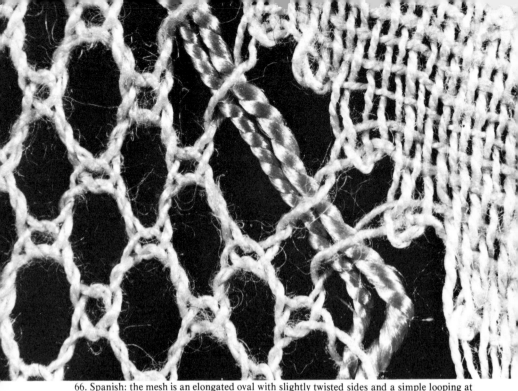

66. Spanish: the mesh is an elongated oval with slightly twisted sides and a simple looping at the top and bottom to produce a small decorative hole. This reseau was found in French blonde of the 1760s and also in some nineteenth-century Russian lace. (13 mm.)

67. Fond simple: a six-sided mesh consisting of four sides twisted twice and two sides crossed. This is from a Bucks lace. Note the small tallies of basket stitch and the silky cordonnet encircling the toilé showing a cut at one point only. (13 mm.)

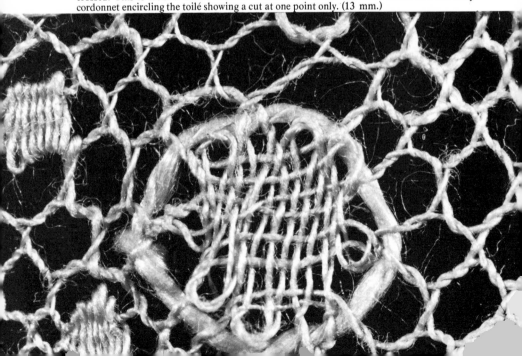

and silver thread beloved of the seventeenth-century Stuart kings. There are also references to gold lace at the burial of the young Edward VI in 1553. Silk thread, both black and white, was sometimes used, as in the gimp lace referred to by Pepys and in the fashionable blonde laces of the late eighteenth and early nineteenth centuries. Silk was very seldom used in needlepoint laces. After 1833, although flax thread was still used, a great deal of bobbin lace was made of the less expensive cotton thread which was 'gassed', that is passed through a flame to make it less fluffy.

The *reseau* (ground, mesh or background) is very important in distinguishing different kinds of bobbin lace. The main types of reseau are: Brussels, Mechlin, Valenciennes, Round Valenciennes, Point de Paris, Cinq Trous, Honeycomb, Torchon, Spanish and Fond Simple. A slightly confusing factor is that some of these reseaux have several different names, for example Point de Paris may also be known as Six Point Star, Fond Chant, Kat Stitch, French Ground and Wire Ground. Another is that a few bobbin laces, mainly late nineteenth-century Brussels ones, have a needlepoint ground. A further factor is that in the course of time the original reseau has in some cases disintegrated, and the toilé may then have been 'regrounded', that is linked together with a reseau of the original type, or alternatively with a different type of reseau, or it may even have been mounted on machine net.

With these four criteria in mind, I shall now examine the various bobbin laces, country by country, in order to show how each can be recognised, identified and distinguished from any other.

(a) ITALIAN BOBBIN LACES

The best known are those from Genoa and Milan in northern Italy. Less important laces were made in Abruzzi in central Italy, and Sicily produced heavy peasant laces.

i. Genoese

This is sometimes known as 'collar lace' as it came into popularity as an edging to the low flat collars of the seventeenth century. It was a smooth solid-looking lace, made of fairly thick thread but closely and evenly worked, and it consisted of a series of scallops like sea shells, joined to a narrow footing. The design was formal and repetitive, and a very distinctive feature was the wheatear decoration. A later slight variation in fashion caused the separate scallops to be joined by a series of short bars. A second type of Genoese was a skeletal lace worked in deliberate imitation of punto in aria and consisting of tooth-like triangles each built up by the plaiting together of four flax threads. Both these types went out of fashion about 1660, probably contemporaneously with the replacement of the collar by the cravat.

68 (above). Genoese, seventeenth century. Two pieces of edging, the upper an imitation of punto in aria. (160 mm.)

69 (top right). An enlargement of the imitation punto in aria (68). With a magnifier the plaited form and short wheatears can be clearly distinguished from the buttonhole outline of genuine punto in aria. (50 mm.)

70 (bottom right). Genoese seventeenth century: an enlargement of a scallop of 'collar lace' showing the heavy thread and very close workmanship, a mixture of plaiting and 'weaving'. (50 mm.)

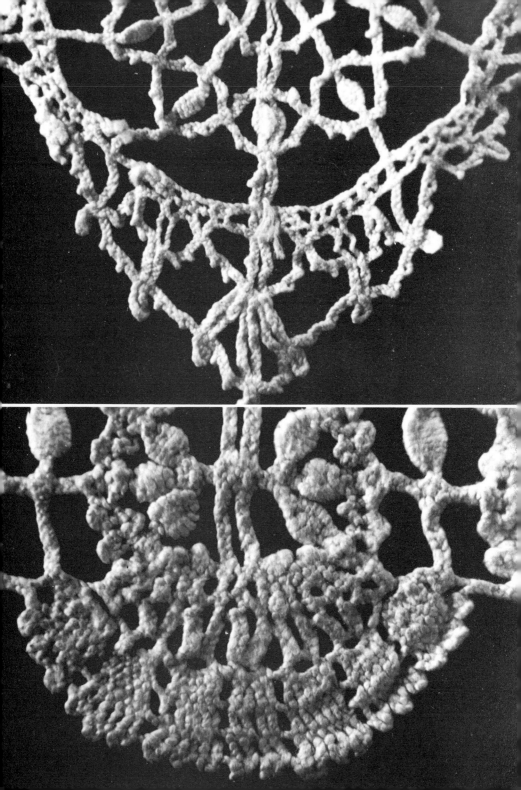

71. Milanese, seventeenth century. The closely packed floral design and very varied fillings are characteristic of this early work of superb quality. (300 mm.)

72. Milanese, late seventeenth century. A small portion enlarged to show the short double brides which are so skilfully joined to the toilé that it looks almost as if the threads are continuous. (50 mm.)

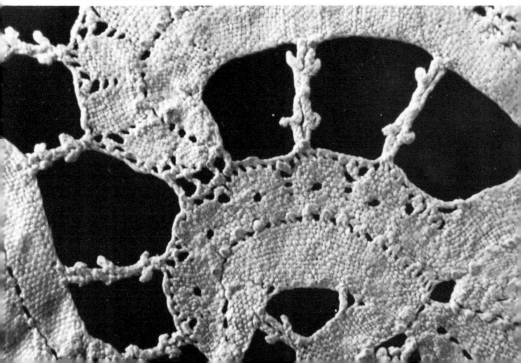

ii. Milanese

This was made from the seventeenth century up to the late eighteenth century and was to some extent revived during the nineteenth century, but its design showed a consistent series of changes over the years and it can be dated with reasonable accuracy. It was made mainly as flounces or entire collars or deep apron edging rather than as fairly narrow edging like Genoese. There was therefore more scope for a fluidity of design and, whereas Genoese was characterised by a static formality, Milanese was boldly sinuous and free-flowing. It had usually no wheatears. The toilé was worked with a middling fine thread, so closely as to resemble a firm linen. The connecting bars were worked separately and in the earliest forms were almost non-existent, the entire lace being made up of glorious flower heads, joined only where they touched, a marvel of design and workmanship to make these individually formed motifs fit so neatly. Around 1700 there were short plaited brides, often arranged in pairs. By the mid eighteenth century the toilé was shrinking and the ground was a reseau of the round Valenciennes type. Where this joined the toilé the threads were frequently carried across the back of the work, a clear indication of the technique. Later, as in other laces, the quality of the design deteriorated and the amount of painstaking but unexciting reseau increased.

The double imperial eagle, that is a two-headed eagle displayed and

73. Milanese, early eighteenth century. The design is good and richly decorated, the reseau of the round Valenciennes type. (360 mm.)

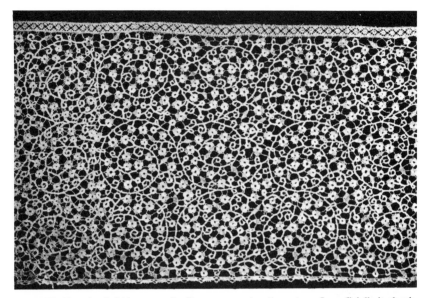

74 and 75. Venetian bobbin, part of a flounce, seventeenth century. Superficially it closely resembles a fine Venetian Point Plat, even to the variations in the tiny flower heads, and it may need a magnifier to distinguish the typical woven appearance of bobbin lace. (380 mm and 120 mm.)

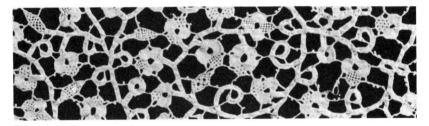

surmounted by a crown, appeared quite commonly on the earlier larger pieces. Although this was associated with the arms of the royal house of Spain, the right to use it was conceded to some Italian families during the time when Milan was part of the Spanish empire, that is until 1714.

iii. Tape laces

These take their name from the fact that the main part of the design appeared as a cursive tape, linked by brides, and filled with a variety of stitches which might be bobbin-made or needlepoint, or in some cases a mixture of fillings would appear in the same length of lace. The tape was either handwoven, straight and narrow, or made by bobbins either as a simple tape or one of extreme complexity, incorporating many variations of width and fillings. A less pretty, indeed rather clumsy-looking, seventeenth-century form has already been referred to on page 25. It used a closely woven straight tape stitched on to a cloth or parchment in its intended snakelike coils and then linked and filled either with bobbin work or with needlepoint stitches, as before. However, because of the stiffness of the tape the changes in direction were marked by awkward overlaps and appeared ragged. Some of these tape laces were made around Genoa and Milan, others near Naples, and also in other parts of Europe.

iv. Venetian bobbin

Brief mention must be made of this rare seventeenth-century lace, which was so closely worked that it looked like a reduced version of the needlepoint Point Plat, with myriads of tiny buds, some pierced with delicate openwork, bursting from thin circinate branches.

v. South Italian and Sicilian peasant laces

These laces, produced from the sixteenth century onwards, were heavy and simple and worked all in one piece instead of, as in Milanese, the separate pieces of toilé and the linking background being independent operations.

Derivatives of these early Italian bobbin laces were:

vi. Maltese

This was made in Malta, and though cotton and linen examples are known the commonest material was a lustrous natural-coloured silk. Black examples were also made, using silk from Barcelona. It was characterised by wheatears copied from the Genoese and by the Maltese Cross. The rest of the design consisted sometimes of very stylised floral or leaf parts or of groupings of highly decorative circles or other geometric figures. The design was repetitive, the reseau plaited, and the lace made all in one piece on a tall pillow which enabled a good length to be produced without too frequent an adjustment of the underlying parchment pattern. The use of thick silk made the work much quicker than with the fine flax of the old Genoese and Milanese. Strips several inches wide were produced, and to make a larger stole, shawl, parasol cover or bedspread the strips were neatly joined, but not always very firmly, and Maltese lace may show splits which make it look as though it is disintegrating when all that has happened is that it has come apart at the

76. Maltese, early twentieth century. This shows the typical Maltese cross, the silk thread, the short fat wheatears and the plaited border. (50 mm.)

seams. The early history of lacemaking in Malta does not appear to be known, but the industry was revived in the 1830s by Lady Hamilton Chichester. A lot of Maltese lace was shown at the Great Exhibition of 1851, and the quality continued to be good until Edwardian times, after which the work became slack and degenerate. Some was made in Genoa.

vii. Bedfordshire Maltese

Because of the enormous popularity of Maltese lace, its general style was copied in England from 1850, producing a type of lace known as Bedfordshire Maltese, said to differ consistently from its prototype in having no Maltese cross and badly made square-ended wheatears instead of neatly pointed ones. Also it was made mainly in white cotton, or when silk was used it was black rather than pale gold. Like Maltese, it was made all in one piece.

(b) DUTCH AND FLEMISH LACES

The geographical boundaries of Flanders during the sixteenth, seventeenth and eighteenth centuries are not easy to determine with any precision, but they may be assumed to have included part of what is now

Belgium, Holland and north-eastern France. Flanders as a political entity disappeared during the time of the French Revolution. 'Flemish' lace is therefore a slightly arbitrary term, but since it is in common use I have grouped together under this head laces named after towns or cities within a 40-mile (65-kilometre) radius of Brussels and which also have some similarity of technique and design.

i. Dutch

This lace is rare and is known only from the seventeenth century. It has a thick strong solid look to it but is in no way clumsy. Its solidity comes not from a coarse flax but from very fine flax, the famous Haarlem thread, worked exceedingly closely. This thread surpassed all others in Europe in the delicacy of its fibre and the silkiness of its gloss. Only seven bast fibres were spun together to make a working thread which measured no more than a twentieth of a millimetre in diameter. The formalised design was distinctive, appearing like rounded bunched bouquets of flower heads not unlike those of the contemporary, or earlier, Dutch still-life paintings. Especially characteristic was the way the pattern repeated on either side of a central line. As in early Milanese, the toilé occupied the greater part of the lace, and there was almost no reseau. It was worked all in one piece.

77. Dutch, seventeenth century. The close texture with almost no ground, the stylised flower heads and the unit of design — a mirror-image repeat about a centre line — are typical. (110 mm.)

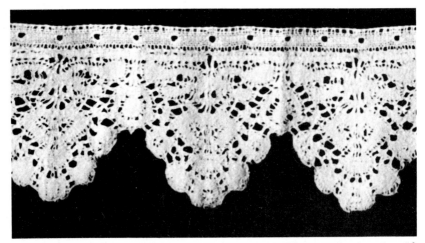

78. Seventeenth-century Flemish. Similar in appearance to Genoese collar lace, but the thread is much finer, the lace softer, and there are no wheatears. (100 mm.)

ii. Seventeenth-century Flemish

Seventeenth-century Flemish lace is known in several forms. One resembled Genoese collar lace in the general shape and the design, which was of repeated shallow scallops each dissected into a kind of fan shape. It differed, however, in the greater fineness of the thread, and in the lack of wheatears. Also, Flanders never produced anything comparable to the Genoese plaited imitation of punto in aria. Another form had very deep beautiful scallops made of filled circles like sections of oranges compressed together. A more loosely textured form was Trolle Kant, not unlike an early Mechlin, with a coarsish cordonnet, a design of somewhat gawky and overgrown flowers, and a reseau of fond d'armure or occasionally cinq trous.

iii. Eighteenth-century Flemish

There are, similarly, forms of Flanders lace which bear only the name 'eighteenth-century Flemish', though they are quite as distinctive as those bearing specific place names (iv-viii). This eighteenth-century Flemish differed strikingly from the earlier form. Toilé and reseau were separately worked, the threads of the reseau being carried across the back of the toilé as in the contemporary Milanese lace, which it so closely resembled as to be sometimes almost indistinguishable. The same round Valenciennes reseau was used, and the same tapelike scrolling, but on the whole the form was less precise. Another kind of eighteenth-century

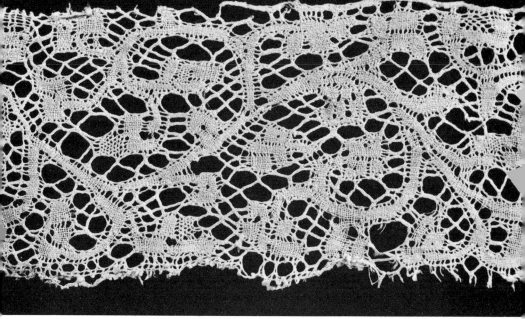

79. Late seventeenth-century Flemish or North German 'peasant lace'; strong, durable and of simple unsophisticated design. (180 mm.)

80. Mid eighteenth-century Flemish. Distinguished from Milanese of the same period by the strangely tortuous design with fragments of toilé linked by sprawling curlicues. Both would have the round Valenciennes reseau but Milanese, even if not well formed, would be more disciplined. This heralds the spotted frivolity of much nineteenth-century Brussels. (330 mm.)

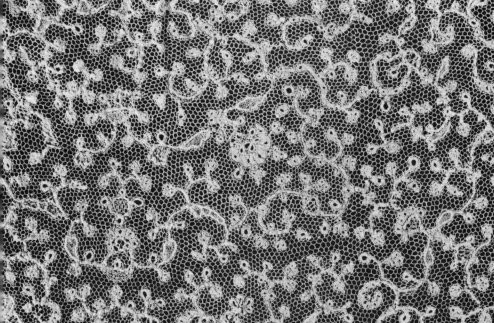

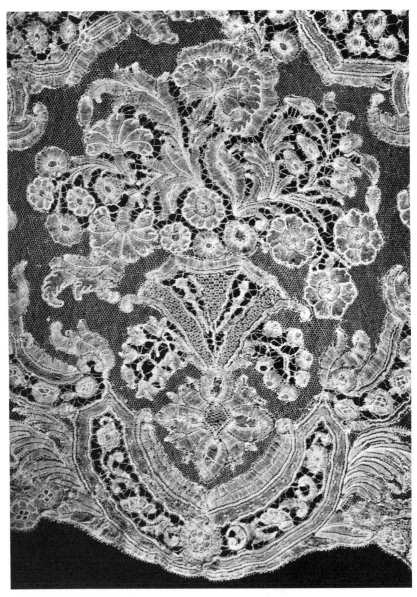

81. Brabant: part of a flounce, mid eighteenth century. A very lovely design with a droschel réseau and typical brides linking the leaves and flower heads. It is loosely textured compared with earlier Flemish laces. (310 mm.)

82. Binche, early eighteenth century. The spotted design is characteristic. (Width of lace 75 mm.)

Flemish existed. In this the toilé was rather broken up and it was difficult to distinguish any pattern, except that occasionally there were tiny scattered winged figures, putti or angels, and here and there voluptuous canopies with people feasting beneath, but all on a very small scale. The reseau too was replaced by brides picotées, a type of background which has been mentioned already under needlepoint laces, but here the brides were plaited by bobbins and not worked over with buttonhole stitch, and also they had no regular arrangement, whereas those of, for example, Point de France were hexagonally formed.

iv. Brabant

The so-called 'eighteenth-century Flemish lace' was made mainly in wide flounces, and so too was Brabant lace, a rather soft loosely worked provincial lace of bold extravagant design linked by short brides. It was used for alb flounces and for cravats but was not a very strong lace, and the thread was probably inferior.

v. Binche

Binche was a gossamer-fine straight-edged lace with a rather indeterminate design of haphazardly scattered spots. Occasionally, though by no means always, a very fine cordonnet was found. The oeil de perdrix fillings and snowflake ground (fond de neige) frequently occurring gave it great charm. There was no other fine lace quite similar to it in design.

vi. Valenciennes

Valenciennes was similar to Binche in its filmy translucent texture but greatly advanced in its lovely designs of gently curving flowers and fronds — carnations were especially favoured — sweeping across the snowflake ground. Like Binche it was worked all in one, but the edge was usually gently curving instead of straight. There was never any cordonnet, but a distinctive characteristic was the continuous line of tiny holes which outlined every part of the toilé. This Valenciennes of the late seventeenth and early eighteenth centuries was an extremely expensive lace because of the very fine thread that was used, which was not only expensive in itself but took an immense time to work; and also because of the vast number of bobbins required by the elaborate design. Only 1½ inches (38 millimetres) per day could be produced, and it would probably take a worker ten months working fifteen hours a day from 4 a.m. to 8 p.m. to complete a pair of men's ruffles, which would then sell for about £14 a yard. The lacemakers were mostly young girls, their hands not roughened by housework, and they laboured in damp cellars so that no dry air should make the thread brittle. Many are said to have become almost blind before they were thirty years old. The fond de neige ground of the early Valenciennes developed, during the late eighteenth century, into the characteristic diamond-shaped reseau plaited on all four sides, which persisted through the nineteenth century, though with very considerable deterioration of quality. The last Valenciennes of real skill was made about 1840.

vii. Antwerp

Antwerp lace in the seventeenth century was similar to Trolle Kant in its somewhat loosely worked texture. It had a cordonnet of strong untwisted thread which appeared disproportionately coarse for the fragile toilé. The reseau was Point de Paris or cinq trous. The best known variety was Potten Kant, so named from the design of a two-handled vase spilling over with flowers in the form of long-stemmed tulips or lilies. In the late eighteenth and early nineteenth centuries it was made as narrow edging or insertion, straight-edged, all in one piece, still with a cordonnet, and characteristically an extensive cinq trous reseau and a simple repetitive blob-like design.

viii. Mechlin

Mechlin, or Malines, lace has been recorded as early as 1657. It was an extremely pretty, almost transparent lace with as much complexity of

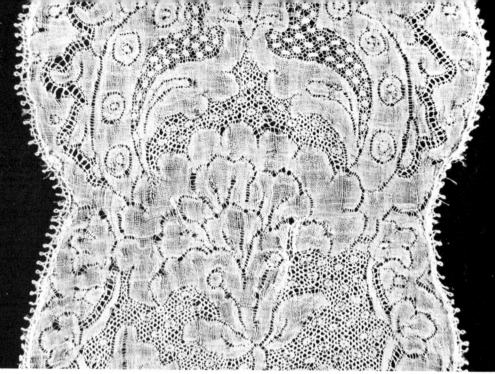

83. Valenciennes: part of a lappet, c. 1700. Note the fine texture and even workmanship. Each part of the toilé is outlined with a row of small dots; the carnation is surrounded by an oeil de perdrix filling, and above is fond de neige ground. A nineteenth-century machine picot has been added. (Width of lappet, 90 mm.)

84. Antwerp, late eighteenth century. This shows a design of a stylised pot of flowers. (100 mm.)

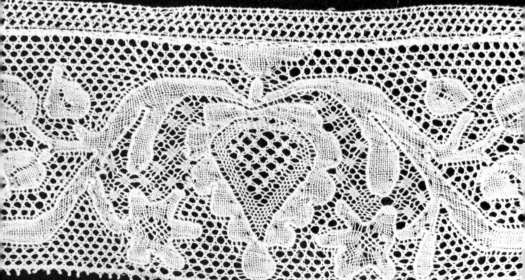

85. Mechlin, seventeenth century, a type of Flemish sometimes called Trolle Kant. A simple lumpy design of a potted plant, and a ground of fond d'armure (armour ground, perhaps from some similarity in appearance to chain mail). (90 mm.)

86. Mechlin, part of a lappet, c. 1700. The reseau occupies a small space in proportion to the toilé. The design and texture are similar to Valenciennes (83), but they can be distinguished by the cordonnet in Mechlin and by the lack of a cordonnet but the presence of an outline of tiny holes in Valenciennes; also by the typical Mechlin reseau where this is present. A nineteenth-century machine picot has been added. (100 mm.)

stitch and richness of design as the early Valenciennes. Also like that lace it had oeil de perdrix fillings and a fond de neige ground. However, it could be distinguished by the presence of a silky cordonnet and the absence of the line of tiny holes around the toilé, so characteristic of Valenciennes. It was made all in one piece, and the heading followed gently the curvature of the design. In 1699 the English prohibition on the importation of Flemish laces was repealed, and by 1713 Mechlin was in very high favour. Queen Anne in that year paid £247 6s 9d for 83 yards (76 metres) of it, or approximately £3 a yard in the currency of that time. Later, in the same way as in other bobbin and needlepoint laces, more and more of the space was taken over by the reseau until by the early nineteenth century the toilé was reduced to a simple floral border of rose sprigs, or even just rose heads, and the reseau was speckled with regularly arranged dots known as point d'esprit. The Mechlin reseau was typically a hexagonal mesh made of two threads twisted twice on four sides and four threads plaited three times on the other two sides, those parallel with the footing.

87. Mechlin, early nineteenth century. A more imaginative design than was usual at this period. (180 mm.)
88. Mechlin. A typical mid nineteenth-century design of simplified roses and scattered sprigs. Both 87 and 88 show an extensive Mechlin reseau. (60 mm.)

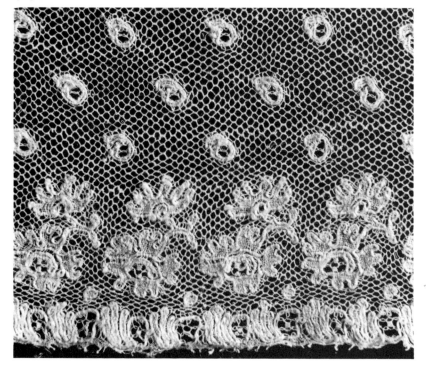

ix. Point d'Angleterre

In this lace the toilé was made separately, and then the joining reseau threads were looped across the back of the design as in eighteenth-century Flemish. Its representations of flowers, people and animals were, however, much more ordered and realistic, sometimes portraying biblical events such as the Annunciation, picturesque hunting scenes with palm trees and Eastern attendants, or exquisitely detailed lilies, carnations, and pomegranates. It resembled Mechlin in the similarity of its reseau, but differed again in having no cordonnet in the sense of a thicker outlining thread, though the edges and veins of the leaves and petals were often built up by slightly raised plaiting. A non-derivative feature was that a light and shade, or perspective, effect was produced by a subtle alternation of wholestitch and halfstitch.

The origin of the name Point d'Angleterre is still a matter for speculation. Some consider it to be a Flemish lace produced at a time when the law prohibiting the importation of foreign laces was being strictly enforced, it being hoped that calling it 'English stitch' would convince the necessary people that it had been made in England. Others consider it to be an English lace, made in the West Country but given a French name because it was based on parchments brought from Flanders by lace workers who settled there, having followed the old wool-trade route between Flanders and Devon.

The early forms, some dating from the late seventeenth century, had no reseau, and the generous and beautiful design filled the entire width of the lace, appearing almost to burst through its edges, as can be seen in some magnificent lappets and cap backs. During the early eighteenth century the very characteristic Flemish or Brussels reseau developed, a hexagonal mesh of which two sides were made of four threads plaited four times (parallel with the footing) and the remaining four sides of two threads twisted twice. Thus it differed from the Mechlin reseau only in having four plaits instead of three. This reseau progressively took over from the toilé until at the end of the eighteenth century a unique innovation occurred — the construction of entire veils, stoles, collars and even skirt flounces consisting only of reseau with no toilé at all. This reseau, known as *vrai reseau* or *droschel*, was very expensive to make, costing between £240 and £500 per pound or £15 per square foot. It could be made only in narrow strips about one inch (25 millimetres) wide, and these had then to be painstakingly joined by an invisible stitch called *point de raccroc*. The work was done so skilfully that even after nearly two hundred years the seams can be seen only if held in a certain light, and then very faintly. It was decorated with appliqué work, the motifs — usually small flowers — being made of Brussels needlepoint or bobbin lace. However Point d'Angleterre did not escape the fate of other hand-

89. Point d' Angleterre: detail of a lappet, early eighteenth century. There is no cordonnet thread as in Mechlin and no consistent outline of tiny holes as in Valenciennes, but there is a raised edging and veining which does not appear in either of the others. The design, however, could be very similar. (100 mm.)

90. Droschel ground, c. 1800, taken with side lighting to show up the faint seams of point de raccroc linking together the narrow strips, about 20 mm, of reseau. Fig. 58 was photographed along one of these joins, but even at that magnification, of about twelve times, the joining is not obvious: it extends across from about the middle of the applied motif.

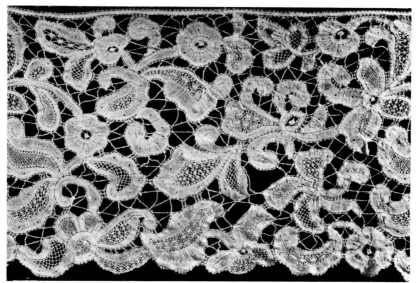

91. Bruges, mid nineteenth century. This is a fine piece, with very varied bobbin fillings. Often it is a much plainer lace though the general design, and the simple brides, are typical. It is coarse, made of cotton, and 360 mm are shown: compare 89, only 100 mm wide, and made of fine flax.

made laces and it deteriorated rapidly during the last decade of the eighteenth century and ceased, along with the droschel ground, in the early nineteenth century.

(c) BRUSSELS LACE

Although Brussels is a city, the term 'Brussels lace' is applied to a variety of laces produced in various parts of Belgium, which was created an independent kingdom in 1833. Thus although some authorities use 'Brussels' and 'Flemish' as interchangeable terms, 'Flemish' should be restricted to eighteenth-century laces, and 'Brussels' to nineteenth-century ones.

The various Brussels laces are described below as sharply distinct types, but they were often made in the same areas, and designs and techniques tended to merge, so that there were many intermediate forms, some of good quality.

i. Bruges

Bruges and the following three types of Brussels lace were called guipure laces, indicating that the separately worked parts of the pattern were held together not by reseau but by brides. Bruges was a white lace of bold but unimaginative design consisting mainly of open flower heads, leaves like elongated trefoils and segmented caterpillars, the brides being stringy and the whole made of coarsish thread, and with a cordonnet.

ii. Duchesse

Duchesse was also a nineteenth-century lace, similar to Bruges in its general lack of fine artistry, but more ornate with relics of the rich eighteenth-century scrolls and arabesques. The cordonnet, when present, was inconspicuous; the leaf veins and borders were raised and plaited or oversewn, and more variety of appearance was achieved by the use of wholestitch and halfstitch.

iii. Mixed

Mixed Brussels was also sometimes called Duchesse, but its distinguishing characteristic was that the bobbin lace was interrupted by medallions of needlepoint usually bearing a small motif such as a flower head.

92. Duchesse, c. 1900. The simple clustered face-on flowers like forget-me-nots, the ribbed leaves and the occasional use of halfstitch are typical. (90 mm.)

93. Brussels mixed lace, c. 1900. The needlepoint medallions are inserted into what is basically a Duchesse lace. The ugly zigzagging brides are typical. (100 mm.)

94. Flemish mixed lace, c. 1750: one hundred and fifty years earlier than 93 and infinitely more delicate and skilled. This shows the reverse side with the threads of the separately attached droschel reseau looping across the neck and tail of the needlepoint peacock. (100 mm.)

95. Rosaline: part of a collar, early twentieth century. The crinkly edges and tiny circular buds are characteristic. (180 mm.)

iv. Rosaline

Rosaline existed in a variety of designs but basically incorporated very simplified rose buds. One distinctive late nineteenth-century form had short wavy-edged tapes linking together tiny flowers, the centres of which were raised and oversewn. In another form the flowers were embedded in a needlemade mesh.

v. Appliqué and embroidered nets

Other types of Brussels lace consisted of machine net decorated with applied bobbin or needlepoint sprigs, or muslin, or embroidered with tambour work in characteristic designs. These are described on pages 113 and 121.

(d) FRENCH BOBBIN LACES

Unlike Brussels, these were made all in one piece. They appear on the whole not to have flourished during the eighteenth century when French needlepoints and Flemish bobbin were so much in vogue, and those which will be described are predominantly nineteenth-century laces.

i. Valenciennes

The city of Valenciennes was annexed by France in 1678, but I have treated the old Valenciennes as essentially Flemish because its design and technique link it so closely with the other Flemish laces (pages 76-85). This fine old Valenciennes reached its peak in the mid eighteenth century, but from 1780, when fashions changed, its decline began. Demand was greatly reduced when cravats and sleeve ruffles ceased to be used as decoration for men's clothes. During the French Revolution the number of lace workers in the city dropped from four thousand to two hundred and fifty, and by 1851 only two were left, both in their eighties. In its heyday only the lace produced within the city was called 'true' or *vrai* Valenciennes; that produced elsewhere was called 'false' or *fausse*. However, great changes took place and during the nineteenth century the monopoly of Valenciennes manufacture was acquired by Belgium. The commercial value of this monopoly was estimated at £800,000. Narrow borders of Valenciennes were much used for trimming underwear and

96. Valenciennes, three nineteenth-century pieces. The upper two share the typical plaited reseau and outline of dots but show extremes of quality. The bottom piece is machine-made, recognisable with a magnifier by the parallel lines in the toilé, and by the impossibility of tracing the threads in the reseau. (180 mm.)

were a favourite of Queen Victoria's on her nightdresses, chemises and open drawers. It was a simple but compact lace, durable and clean-looking, the decoration being of round dots or small stylised flowers. The clothwork was smooth and even, with an edging of minute holes as in the eighteenth-century form; the reseau was diamond-shaped and plaited on all four sides.

ii. Lille

Although geographically the city of Lille is very near Valenciennes and the old Flemish border, its lace was of the simple French style, being mostly reseau of the fond simple type, that is four sides twisted twice and two sides crossed. It often appeared cloudy, this being the result, as in Burano needlepoint, of the unevenness of the cotton thread. Unlike Valenciennes it had a cordonnet, and the simple looping of this alongside the heading was often the only design that appeared, so that there was no distinct toilé. This was a very characteristic feature of Lille, another being that the heading was almost invariably straight.

97. A simple but beautifully made Valenciennes edging to the sleeve of a chemise of the young Queen Victoria. The material is superlative linen, every seam stitched minutely by hand. (260 mm.)

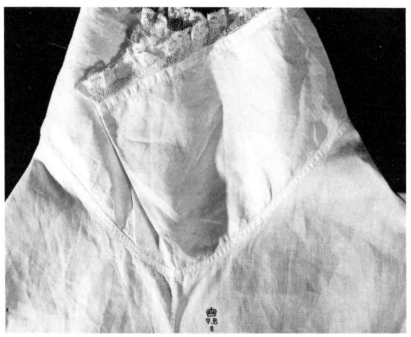

98. Lille, second half of the nineteenth century. The point d'esprit in the fond simple reseau and the design formed by the looped and branched cordonnet, rather than by a distinct toilé, are characteristic. (110 mm.)

99. Chantilly: part of a fan leaf, late nineteenth century. The naturalistic representation, of putti alighting from a barque, of bulrushes and Solomon's seal, are typical, as are the predominance of halfstitch, the fond simple reseau, and the flat untwisted cordonnet. (230 mm.)

iii. Chantilly

This was a mainly black lace, though white examples are known dating from the early nineteenth century. It is said that production flourished between 1740 and 1785 when it was under the patronage of Louis XV (1715-74) and Louis XVI (1774-93), but few eighteenth-century examples have been identified. This may be because the black dye which was used was acid and contained iron. It tended to oxidise, lose its colour and rot the fabric. Like other French laces it declined with the Revolution (1789-95), but it was revived about 1804 by the Emperor Napoleon I, who decreed that only Alençon and Chantilly laces should be worn at court. It was made of varying qualities until Edwardian times. As with other laces made in one piece, the possible width of each strip was limited by the size of the pillow and the difficulty of manoeuvring the bobbins; thus as in droschel and Maltese, large items such as stoles, capes or shawls had to be made of smaller pieces invisibly stitched together. Even fascinators, fall caps and fan leaves required some joining. The main designs were floral, with pleasantly naturalistic roses, tulips, daffodils and irises, with swags and ribbons, and occasionally birds, putti or grape and vine leaves with tendrils. The earlier Chantilly was made of flax but all the later was of a dull grenadine silk stiffened with gum arabic. The toilé was usually of halfstitch and was continuous with the fond simple, or occasionally Point de Paris, reseau. The cordonnet consisted of several strands of flat untwisted silk. In 1870 the firm became bankrupt, but similar if rather coarser laces were still produced elsewhere, for example at Calvados, Caen, Bayeux and Le Puy and also a form of not very good quality in Buckinghamshire, where it was known as 'Amersham Black'.

iv. Caen

Caen also gave its name to a lustrous silk lace of an ivory colour. The texture was fairly close, and the toilé of a denser silk than the fond simple reseau. The design was often a simple floral one like open daisy heads or ears of barley and was outlined with a thick silk strand. Some authorities say that Caen was first made about 1745 and that this eighteenth-century form sometimes had a cordonnet of chenille or of gold thread. Caen was usually made in the summer because it was easier then to keep the delicate colour clean and the silk smooth and unruffled by chafed hands. Caen was called a white blonde lace.

v. Le Puy

Le Puy also had a characteristic lace which bears its name, although a great variety of laces were produced in the town. This was a black lace of

100. White Chantilly: a mitten, early nineteenth century. Basically it has all the characteristics of the far commoner black Chantilly. (230 mm.)

101. Caen, nineteenth century. The naturalistic design is more delicate than Chantilly and the silk much softer. This piece shows the skilful combination of thicker threads with wholestitch, and finer threads with half-stitch, to give a striking contrast of light and shade. (230 mm.)

silk or cotton, sometimes called a guipure because of the characteristic ground of brides picotées, grouped into alternating hexagons and triangles, though it was made all in one piece, the larger flounces or shawl collars being composed of joined fragments. The design was open with bold lines enclosing cartouches of glossy halfstitch or fond simple, sometimes worked with a finer thread. Often too there were rosettes or feather-like rows of wheatears and a scalloped heading of fine plaits.

vi. Normandy

Normandy laces, as far as they had any distinctive features, were of a childlike simplicity and charm. One was Ave Maria, which consisted only of a Valenciennes ground and a row of small dots next to a picot edge. It was often made in very narrow widths and used for babies' bonnets. Dieppe also was a kind of Valenciennes, slightly coarse, but closely and firmly worked, with a very simplified short-repeat design. Dentelle à la Vierge was more interesting, the design consisting of regularly arranged quatrefoils, each surrounded by a cordonnet, and embedded in a cinq trous reseau.

(e) SPANISH LACES

The most distinctive type is the so-called Spanish bobbin, which was used mainly for mantillas and stoles. The material was a glistening black silk, which was softer and more fragile than that of Chantilly. The design was a floral one of petals, or even flower sprays, with a cordonnet around the clothwork, and occasional honeycomb fillings. The reseau was fond simple and was made in one with the toilé. As in other all-in-one laces, the larger articles had to be made up of strips, invisibly joined. Although the colour was black, this is classified as a blonde lace because it was made of silk. A shiny white version, of similar design, was also made during the nineteenth century, though in much smaller quantities. Although many other types of bobbin lace were made in Spain during both the eighteenth and nineteenth centuries, 'Spanish bobbin' is the only one which does not appear to have been produced in large quantities elsewhere. A coarse form of both black and white Chantilly was made in Barcelona.

102. Le Puy, late nineteenth century. Although there is an appearance of plaited brides with picots, this lace is not a guipure but made all in one piece. The formal design, cartouches of 'net stitch' and rows of wheatears are typical. (150 mm.)

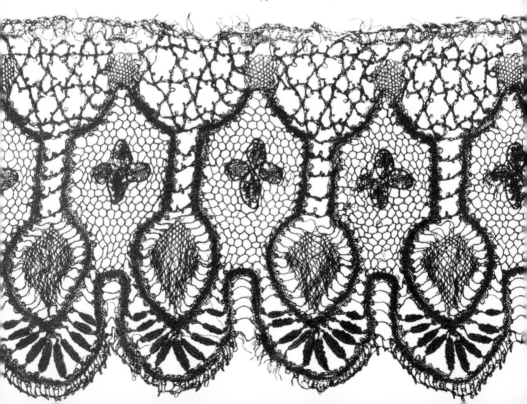

103. Spanish bobbin, nineteenth century. The closely worked flower petals of heavy silk bordering the lace and edged with picots are typical, also the honeycomb fillings, the cordonnet — visible around the halfstitch — and the fond simple reseau appearing rather irregular because of the springiness of the silk. (110 mm.)

104. A larger piece of Spanish bobbin to show a typical design, taken from a mantilla which was made in strips 75-100 mm wide. A clear join is visible where the texture of the silks was not perfectly matched. (200 mm.)

(f) ENGLISH BOBBIN LACES

As in the other European countries the varieties of bobbin lace by district and design are innumerable, and so only the more distinctive ones will be described here and the names used will be taken to refer to types rather than to precise places of origin. The two main groups are Honiton and Midlands laces. While both owe some influence to the Flemish refugees of the sixteenth century, this was overlaid in the Midlands by the later influx of French Huguenots. Thus Honiton more closely resembles Flemish and Brussels laces, while Midlands laces show similarities with France.

i. Honiton

As in the Brussels laces, the technique in Honiton was to make the toilé separately and then to fix the design in position either by bobbin-made brides, sometimes with picots, or with a needlemade reseau of the Alençon type, or with a bobbin reseau which could be of a complex leaded form or of the simpler net-stitch. In few cases, however, were the background threads carried across the reverse side of the work as they were in Flemish and Milanese. The designs were typically of neatly worked roses, thistles, shamrocks and butterflies, with a variety of fillings such as

105. Part of a rare eighteenth-century Honiton flounce, the droschel ground at odd angles, not neatly parallel as in the Brussels form (figs. 58, 90, 94). (180 mm.)

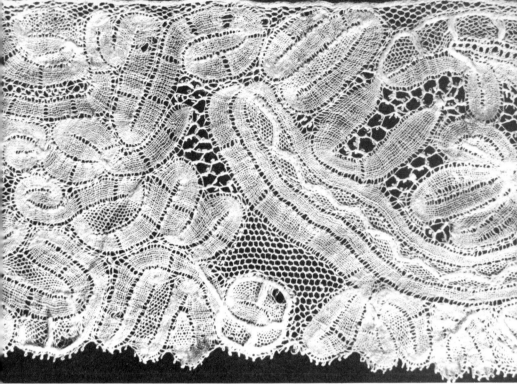

106. A piece of late eighteenth-century Devon edging showing the 'worn-out' design, and with some haphazard raising of the edges. The droschel ground is again at an angle. (90 mm.)

107. Honiton with net-stitch ground: part of a collar, c. 1840. The typical design of rose, thistles and shamrock is clearly defined, and plaited fillings and roll and tie edging can be seen. (200 mm.)

108. Honiton: a cuff, late nineteenth-century revival. The toilé is linked by brides with picots. The technique was first used in the early 1840s. (90 mm.)

cucumber, toad in the hole, blossom, snatchpin and so forth. Sometimes the toilé was entirely of wholestitch, sometimes halfstitch was also used; sometimes there was a silky cordonnet, sometimes a roll and tie edge as if Brussels was imitating Honiton. The material was nearly always cotton rather than flax, and no silk examples are known. Although there seems no doubt that lace was made in south Devon as far back as the seventeenth century, there appears to be not a single documented piece which can with certainty be ascribed to that time, so that we have no idea precisely what kind of lace was produced then, though it was referred to as 'bone' lace. A few eighteenth-century flounces are known of a bold floral design, but also a much finer narrower form with the droschel reseau so characteristic of the enigmatic Point d'Angleterre, though in many cases the design was both simpler and less well defined, as though the parchments from which it was made were too well worn. These pieces, appearing sometimes as lappets and cap backs, are often called 'Devon' lace. In the early nineteenth century there was a decline in Honiton lacemaking. However, Queen Adelaide, wife of William IV, Queen Victoria and later Queen Alexandra and Queen Mary all encouraged lacemaking in the Honiton area, and there were various revivals, the last around 1880 when designs of a Brussels type with rose blossoms and leaves, with raised edges and veins, were produced. In the second half of the nineteenth century Honiton motifs were prettily applied to machine nets to make collars, cuffs, fichus, scarves and wedding veils. The motifs were pinned in place on a cloth and the net was stretched over

109. Poor-quality Honiton appeared at intervals over a hundred years, between revivals. It was loose, of careless design and inferior cotton, with even some machine tape inserted at the top to give firmness to the collar. The shapeless fragments are called locally slugs and snails. (180 mm.)

them, that is they were stitched through from the back. For more detail of this history I recommend the booklet *Honiton Lace* published by Exeter Museum. The museum in Honiton itself has a pricking for a handkerchief ordered by Queen Adelaide; and Buckland Abbey has some very fine Honiton pieces designed and executed by members of the Tucker family, including a royal coat of arms made for the Great Exhibition of 1851. According to local legend Thomas Tucker, the lace merchant and brilliant designer, was a tyrant who forced his daughters to work the lace until, when at last he died, their resentment flared up and they made a bonfire of all his prickings.

ii. Midlands

Midlands was the group name given to the other main type of English lace. It included those laces made in the counties of Buckingham, Bedford and Northampton and, because of general similarities of design and technique, Wiltshire and Suffolk. They aimed at a modest market, unlike Honiton, which at its best could compete with the fine Brussels laces for the patronage of the rich. They were essentially both light and practical, made all in one piece, and were mainly fairly narrow edgings and insertions between ¼ inch and 4 inches (6-100 millimetres) wide. Not many

110. Honiton motifs applied to three-twist net, which is then cut away behind the flower centres, which have diamond leadwork and brick fillings. Second half of the nineteenth century. (200 mm.)

111. Torchon, early twentieth century, showing the geometric pattern at 45 degrees to the footing, the torchon reseau and small tallies. (75 mm.)

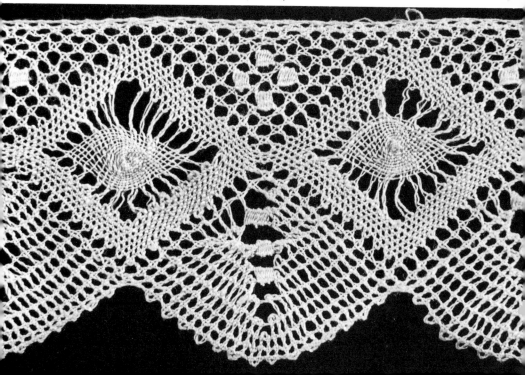

large pieces are known, but there are a few stoles, capes and shawl collars. Several main types can be distinguished:

Torchon was a simple lace, the name being derived from the French word for rag or duster, and it was sometimes known as Beggars' Lace because it was quick to make and cheap to produce. It is thought to have originated in Saxony and France. The material was a firm cotton or flax, the design geometric, but nevertheless with an astonishing variety of patterns, some of them very pretty. The pattern was always at 45 degrees to the footing. A reseau, if clearly present, was of the torchon type, and there was usually no cordonnet.

Yak in design was a kind of torchon lace made of wool, with geometrical motifs, a simple torchon or cinq trous reseau and no cordonnet. Often it had a scalloped edge and raised wheatears. It was introduced in 1870 and used to trim christening capes and children's winter dresses. Not much is found now because of the ravages of moths and, doubtless for the same reason, it did not remain fashionable for very long. Also it was difficult to work as the threads tended to catch and drag on each other instead of gliding smoothly as flax or gassed cotton would do.

112. Yak, late nineteenth century. Characterised by the strong lustrous wool of which it was made, though the white form is usually dull. This example has a cinq trous ground. (150 mm.)

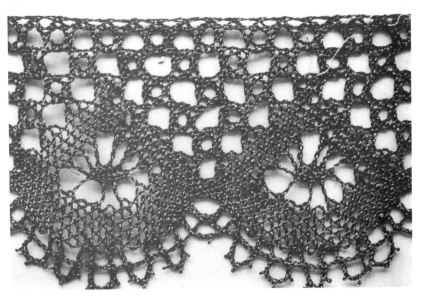

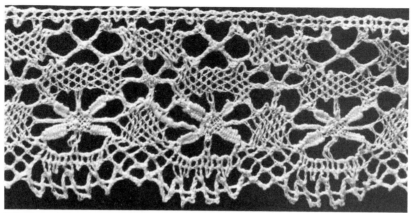

113. Cluny, early twentieth century, showing the characteristic design of radiating wheatears and plaited border. (80 mm.)

Cluny also originated from France and was a heavy plaited lace of geometric design, often with radiating wheatears. It appeared in the nineteenth century, using designs based on the sixteenth-century laces in the Museum of Antiquities at the Hotel Cluny, Paris. The border was of the simple six-pin form, in contrast to the more elaborate, though also plaited, nine-pin border of Beds Maltese and Maltese. Further, the arrangement of the passive threads made it possible for Cluny to have a divided trail, while Beds Maltese could not. It was used mainly as a furnishing lace.

Bucks is the common abbreviation for Buckinghamshire lace. It had usually a fond simple reseau and a coarse silky cordonnet around the toilé of wholestitch. There were varied fillings, for example honeycomb stitch. The reseau was worked in diagonal lines from the footing towards the heading. The design was not geometric but representational in a provincial manner of simple flowers, fruits and other country objects and the various patterns had entrancing rustic names such as Peacock's Tail, Acorn, Rose and Tulip, Carnation, Earring, Seashell, Beehive and Wedding Bell, some very complex and requiring up to five hundred bobbins. Mostly cotton was used, though occasional silk pieces are found; for example in the 1860s Caen blonde was imitated, and the surviving eighteenth-century pieces are of flax thread. Some early nineteenth-century wedding veils were made with a net centre of the two-twist bobbin type which not only imitated exactly the crossing and twisting of the fond simple reseau but had the weft worked diagonally — that is it was said to be traversed. To this the Bucks border was so neatly joined that it was

114. Bucks, an eighteenth-century stocking front. The designs are simple and typical, as are the fond simple reseau scattered with groups of point d'esprit, the honeycomb fillings and the silky cordonnet. The toilé is never so much reduced as in Lille. (120 mm.)

115. Bucks. A typical nineteenth-century design. (100 mm).

difficult to tell where the handmade lace ended and the machine-made began. There were a few Bucks imitations of Mechlin lace, though in Bucks the threads twist before passing out from the toilé to embrace the cordonnet and continue into the reseau, while in true Mechlin they do not. Some Bucks designs show a striking similarity to early Lille ones, having been influenced by parchments brought over by refugees from the French Revolution. Wheatears are never found in Bucks laces.

Downton. The laces of Downton in Wiltshire are very similar to the torchon and Bucks laces described above and in their finished product the origin cannot be identified. Over a hundred different designs are known, but it would need lengthy and arduous research into each of these before any reliable place of origin might be uncovered. In the technique of making, however, there is an intriguing variation in that Downton is worked with the footing on the left of the pillow as in continental laces, while Bucks is worked with the footing on the right, which might perhaps suggest that the Downton industry was started by French or Flemish workers settling there. On the other hand this practice could be a relatively recent introduction by a teacher trained on the continent. Another point of difference, said to be consistent, is that whereas in Bucks a handkerchief border would be made in the shape of a square, the corners right-angled, in Downton the handkerchief border would be

116. Beds Maltese: part of a collar, second half of the nineteenth century. It shows the nine-pin border, the plaited ground with picots and the pleasing combination of geometric and floral design. (200 mm.)

117. An enlargement of a small portion of Beds Maltese to show the square-ended tallies and the plaited border. (50 mm.)

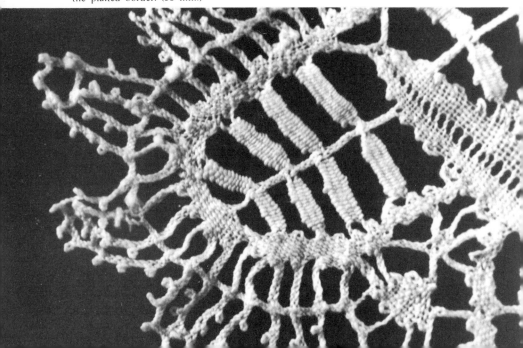

118. Beds 'plaited' lace. Confusion arises from the double meaning of the word 'plaited' either as in the border in 117, or as a synonym for tallies or point d' esprit, made technically by basket stitch, not plaiting. A silky thread passing through the middle of the toilé is characteristic of this lace. (170 mm.)

gathered at the corners as if it were initially a straight piece of edging adapted for that purpose. Typically, too, the pillow on which the lace was worked was bolster-shaped in Downton, cushion-shaped in Bucks; also Downton bobbins had no spangles to weight them, but they were slightly larger and shaped like Honiton bobbins, while Bucks bobbins had spangles, the thread being perhaps a little coarser and so needing a heavier pull on it.

Bedfordshire Maltese was a variety made around the 1850s to compete with the very popular laces imported from Malta. It was made in black silk or white cotton and has already been described on page 76 as an indirect derivative of the Italian bobbin laces. The brides which formed the ground were sometimes known locally as 'legs'. A late nineteenth-century variety of Beds Maltese of superlative quality was that designed by Thomas Lester (1835-1909), portraying either beautiful and realistic flowers or exotic creatures such as emus, giraffes, eagles and stags. An excellent collection of these can be seen at the Cecil Higgins Museum in Bedford. In other forms of Beds a large rose and leaf design occurred linked by a sparse torchon ground.

Plaited lace is perhaps a misnomer for a rare type of Bedfordshire lace where the ground is filled with a trelliswork of square-ended tallies (see Glossary) rather like the leadwork background of a few Honiton pieces. The flower and leaf design extends almost across the width of the lace, and more of the small tallies occur as fillings.

By the second half of the nineteenth century machines had managed to imitate very successfully all the Midlands laces and so inevitably the more expensive handmade products declined. This process was accelerated by the education laws, which led to the closure of the child-employing lace schools between 1871 and 1880.

(g) EAST EUROPEAN LACES

I shall treat these as a group. They include Russian, Hungarian, Czechoslovakian and German (Saxony) laces, none of which are found at all commonly in Britain. Made all in one piece, they were of formalised rather than naturalistic design. The first three were characterised by sinuous symmetrical curves, not unlike snails or sections through a sea anemone or budding Hydra, and by a heading of small closely worked scallops following the convolutions of the design. Colours were often worked into the lace, red and blue being the commonest, for example in Russia and Czechoslovakia. Reseau or fillings were often clearly present and could be of the torchon, cinq trous or honeycomb variety. Saxony was well known for a kind of torchon lace, with a cordonnet around blocks of halfstitch and a short repeat. The material was usually cotton or flax, but occasionally silk. Saxony also made excellent copies of eighteenth-century droschel, and a Brussels bobbin lace with relief work in needlepoint was made there too. Some of their imitations were sold as genuine antique laces.

119. Russian, eighteenth century. The U-bend curving of the tapelike toilé is characteristic. (180 mm.)

4. Machine laces and other 'imitation' laces

The early history of machine net has been recounted in the section on the history of lace, pages 7-20. Heathcoat's bobbin net, invented in 1808, was similar to a fond simple reseau such as is found in Bucks or Lille hand-made bobbin lace, that is it consisted of a hexagonal mesh with four sides twisted twice and two sides crossed over. It could be made in much larger pieces than hand reseau which was limited by the size of the pillow; and also, on the whole, it was more even. It can be distinguished, therefore, by there being no joins and by its greater regularity, though this became less obvious with wear.

Other nets imitated the Point de Paris reseau and droschel, but the diamond mesh of 1831 and after, which was also known as Brussels net or three-twist net, had no handmade equivalent. The novelty of John Heath-coat's bobbin net was found to be so attractive in those days, when the fashion was for simplicity, that it was sometimes used plain for shawls, collars and cuffs, or even for whole dresses.

(a) DECORATED NETS

Very shortly afterwards, however, it was used as the basis for a rapidly expanding industry of decorated nets, first at Nottingham and then in Ireland, and thousands of workers were employed. Designs were block-printed on the net and then embroidered by hand either by chain stitch or by a darning stitch. The first was called tambour work.

i. Tambour work

This was done with a steel-ended tambour needle, rather like a miniature crochet hook, and the chain stitch can easily be identified. The work done in Ireland is sometimes called 'Limerick tambour', and the designs were usually of simple floral whorls or sprays, sometimes with harps and shamrocks. Though they were delicate and charming, there was an angularity and slight awkwardness about them. Tambour work was also done in Belgium, using a thicker thread and a more elaborate, sometimes overcrowded and fussy design. In this 'Brussels tambour' the net, typically, was spotted with little tambour circles and the borders of the net were scalloped, whereas in Limerick they were more often straight.

Another centre of tambour work was Coggeshall in Essex. The net characteristically used there had the hexagonal rather than the diamond-shaped mesh. The industry is thought to have been started by a French-man who settled in Coggeshall in the first quarter of the nineteenth century, that is before the three-twist Brussels net was invented.

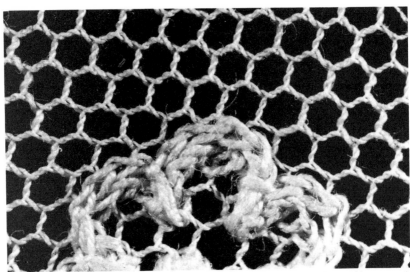

120. Heathcoat's two-twist bobbin net with four sides twisted twice and two sides crossed. The tambour (chainstitch) decoration shown here helps to pinpoint it as machine-made — a hand-made reseau would be far too expensive to be used for embroidery. (10 mm.)

121. Heathcoat's three-twist bobbin net with four sides twisted three times and two sides crossed. There is no handmade equivalent, and the net is easily recognisable by its diamond-shaped mesh and light clear appearance. Here, a fragment of applied needlepoint is visible, and this lace would be known as 'Brussels needlepoint appliqué'. (9 mm.)

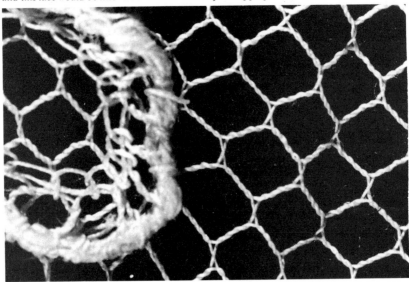

122. A juxtaposition of fond simple and two-twist net. The lower border is Lille, joined along its footing to the net. The photograph is of the reverse side and shows the very neat joining and the trimming back of the net, so that from the right side the junction of machine-made and hand-made is invisible. (140 mm.)

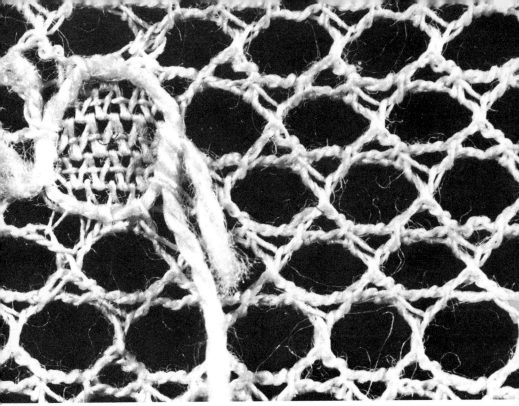

123 (above). Machine Point de Paris. A very good imitation, but the six triangles are not sharply clear and the individual threads are mussed together and cannot be followed through. At the same time the stretched longitudinal lines stand out in parallel sequence (compare 62). The cordonnet has cut ends on each side (compare 67). The toilé threads appear looped rather than woven, and the continuity of thread between toilé and reseau is clumsy (compare 66). (13 mm.)

124 (top right). Machine droschel: part of a bonnet veil, mid nineteenth century. The plaiting is extremely skilful, but over a larger area — this photograph shows no more than 13 mm — the precise regularity of each row gives an impression of parallel bars which must make one suspect a mechanical origin. Also there are no joins as would be necessary in droschel (fig. 90), and it has been used as a ground for Carrickmacross appliqué — the muslin on the right is bound with an overstitched cordonnet. Real droschel would be too expensive for this treatment. One square foot of net in the 1850s cost only 15d, while the same area of droschel cost £15.

125 (bottom right). Machine Mechlin. This is a shade less convincing than the machine droschel because of the clumsy twisting of the threads at the sides (compare 59). The cordonnet cut in several places is also clumsy, and again in the toilé the effect is of looping not weaving. (13 mm.)

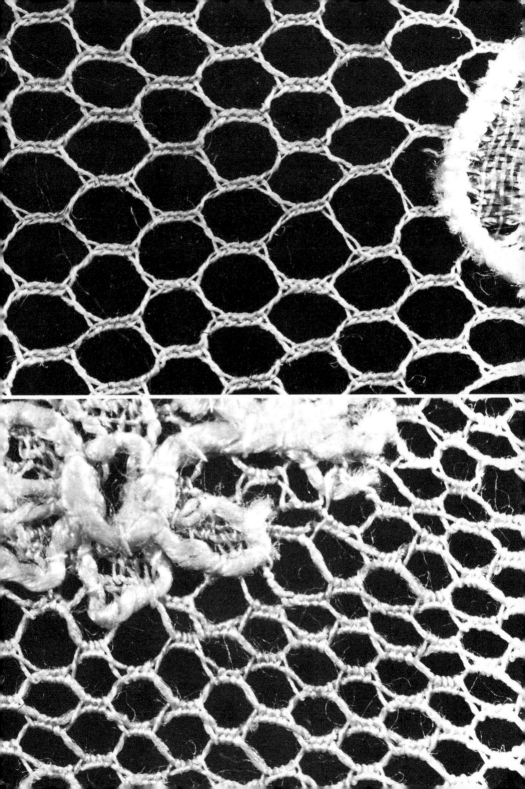

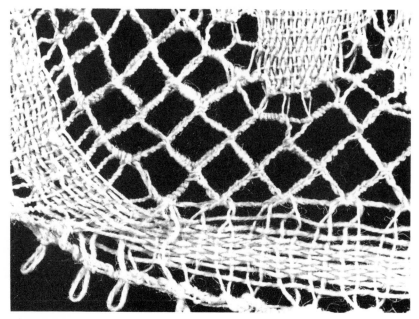

126. Machine Valenciennes. This can be deceptive from a distance especially if compared with an inferior piece of bobbin Valenciennes where the plaiting is badly done. The outlining row of holes is there, and even a fairly convincing woven toilé, but with a magnifier the general tangled appearance of the threads and the impossibility of following each one make the machine origin clear. (13 mm.)

ii. Needlerun

Needlerun, or darned net, is sometimes called 'Nottingham lace', but this is a very confusing term in view of the great variety of laces which over the last one hundred and fifty years have emanated from that city. It can be distinguished from similar patterning produced by machine by the fact that the darning thread can be seen quite clearly ducking in and out of the meshes of the net, and from handmade laces of similar design by the presence of net within the design, by the cordonnet (see page 129) and by the separately attached machine picot with which it was usually trimmed.

The Limerick form, transferred to Ireland from Nottingham in 1829, was often of two thicknesses of thread and had flower fillings presenting a whole variety of ingenious stitches. It was used for wedding veils, poke bonnet veils, stoles, collars and fichus. A much thicker needlerun, in silk rather than cotton thread, is still made in Spain, especially for small triangular scarves used as head coverings or token mantillas. A very coarse

127. Tambour work, mid nineteenth century. Chain stitch on two-twist bobbin net. Either Limerick or Coggeshall. (100 mm.)

128. Needlerun, mid nineteenth century. Darning stitch on three-twist bobbin net. Note the continuity of the net through the design and the design itself formed simply by darning in and out of the meshes in a variety of stitches. (50 mm.)

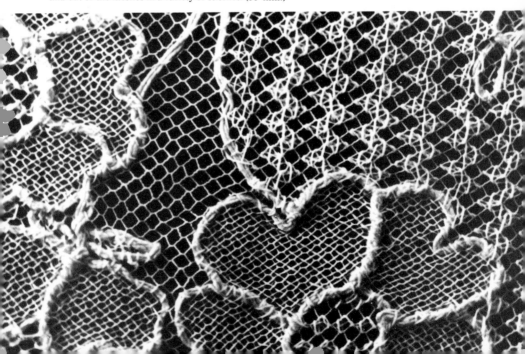

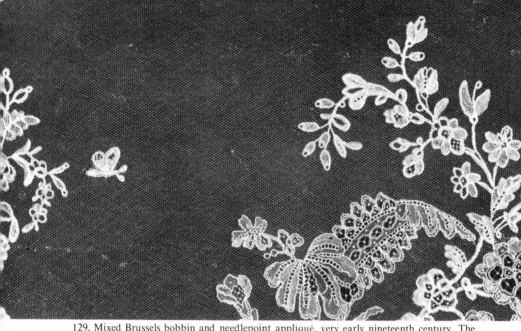

129. Mixed Brussels bobbin and needlepoint appliqué, very early nineteenth century. The ground is droschel. Though this was never used for embroidery or the coarser 'imitation' laces, it was used for the application of very fine hand-made motifs. (290 mm.)

130. Net on net, late nineteenth century. Recognisable with a magnifier as two layers of net joined together by an outline of chainstitch, though from a short distance it can resemble either a needlepoint appliqué or a fine needlerun. The spots indicate a Brussels origin. (200 mm.)

needlerun lace made by Belgian immigrants (the fifth exodus of lacemakers from the continent to England) after the First World War was used mainly on the underwear of the 1920s.

iii. Appliqué work
Honiton and Brussels appliqué

The use of machine net as a background for the application of Honiton or Brussels bobbin or needlepoint sprays has already been mentioned (pages 92 and 103). It was quite common for women to buy one spray a week, or as they could afford it, and when they had enough to stitch them, using their own design, to a piece of net. The invention of machine net was therefore to some extent an advantage to Honiton lacemaking.

Other forms of appliqué work were:

Net on net

This was made mainly in Brussels. Two layers of net were arranged over a pattern, stitched together around the outline of the design either by hand or, in the second half of the nineteenth century, by machine, and then the surplus of the upper net was trimmed away, leaving a pretty design, which might, at a casual glance, be mistaken for a needlepoint appliqué.

131. Carrickmacross, mid nineteenth century. Recognisable by the pieces of muslin cloth bound down by an overstitched cordonnet and by the exposed net of the flowers decorated with darning stitch designs. Here the ground is machine droschel (124), but both two-twist and three-twist bobbin net were also used. (50 mm.)

Carrickmacross

In the work that goes by this name a similar method was used, but the upper layer was of translucent muslin, instead of net. It was made from about 1830 into the twentieth century. The pattern was drawn in ink on glazed linen or card, then covered with a layer of net, then with the muslin. A cordonnet thread was oversewn to outline the individual pieces of the design, and then the surplus muslin was cut away, leaving flowers, leaves or other motifs applied to the net. The centres of the flowers, where the net was exposed, were then filled with varied embroidery stitches, as in the best needlerun. Sometimes in Carrickmacross work the net was dispensed with. The stitching was then applied to the muslin alone, and the outline threads were linked by brides to form, after the removal of the surplus muslin, a Carrickmacross guipure. Some of the flounces and capes produced in this way are quite superb, but it was not a practical lace because shrinkage of the material during washing caused it to pull away from its outlining thread, leaving unsightly gaps. It was also extraordinarily difficult to iron.

Brussels or Belgian muslin appliqué

In this form the cotton material used was too opaque for any design to show through from below, and so the pattern was printed or pounced on the fabric itself instead of being behind the net. Net and fabric were then stitched together along this line using the chainstitch machine. Finally, as in net on net and Carrickmacross the excess fabric was cut away by hand, leaving the design attached to the net. There were few fillings, and it lacked the delicacy and craftsmanship of its Irish counterpart, but it could look spectacularly impressive as a wedding veil, jacket or negligée.

The muslin in Carrickmacross and Brussels muslin appliqué, like the upper net in net on net, was replacing bobbin or needlepoint motifs and thus saving a lot of time and money. Much of the lacemaking effort of the nineteenth century was directed towards this end. Even so, as the machine-patterned laces became more and more perfected, the embroidered nets became less and less commercially viable, and in the later nineteenth century most of the work was carried out not in factories but by isolated amateurs or in convents.

(b) MACHINE-PATTERNED LACES

Five main types of machine were used in the making of laces during the nineteenth century, and four of these have continued production into modern times. They are the Warp Frame, Bobbin Net, Pusher, Levers and Lace Curtain machines.

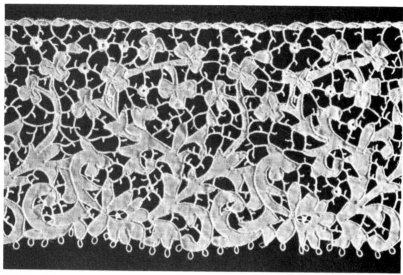

132. Carrickmacross guipure, nineteenth century. No net was used, only muslin outlined and cut, as in 131, then linked by brides. The shamrocks indicate an Irish origin. (130 mm.)

133. Brussels muslin appliqué, c. 1900. The muslin attached to the underlying net is distinguished from Carrickmacross by the chainstitch edging, the opaque cloth and the careless cutting away of the material so that rough edges are left. (100 mm.)

i. The Warp Frame

The Warp Frame was invented about 1775 as a development of the Stocking Frame. This had been worked in much the same way as hand-knitting, the looped stitches going straight across in horizontal rows from a continuous thread, as from a ball of wool. It shared not only the technique but also the disadvantage of hand-knitting in that it could ladder and unravel. The Warp Frame overcame this difficulty: the stocking-stitch rows, instead of passing horizontally across the fabric, were vertical; also the threads which made up these rows were separate instead of continuous, but at the same time the threads were able to loop across from one vertical row to another, locking them together. This technique enabled patterning to take place by leaving the vertical rows unconnected in parts, forming a firm hole, and the earliest patterned Warp Frame laces were known as bullet-hole nets.

Warp Frame lace was popular for blonde edgings in the 1820s and for mittens, veils and shawls, all mainly in silk. Simple needlerun designs

134. Warp Frame derivative. This is the back of the lace showing the basic arrangement of vertical rows of loops with occasional cross-connections. The patterning is produced by the attachment of other threads to the surface. (153 mm.)

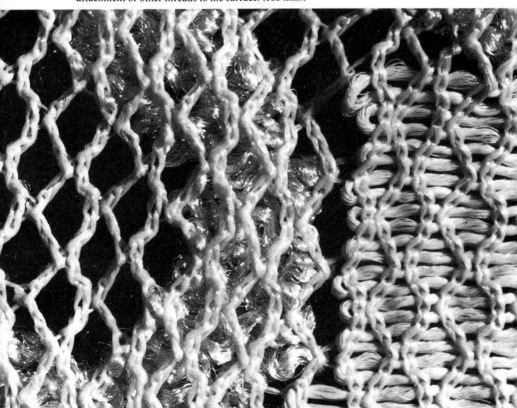

135. The use of the Jacquard apparatus, showing how even a complex design, such as the Nottingham Council House, can be exactly repeated. (Width of lace 230 mm.)

decorated the fairly plain net, and the outlining thread or cordonnet continued to be run in by hand until the mid 1840s, after which it was done by the machine. The Jacquard apparatus was used from the 1830s.

A small amount of Warp Frame net — sometimes called 'point net', presumably from some resemblance to a needlemade reseau — survives from the late eighteenth century, and some patterned laces from the first half of the nineteenth century, but it is fairly rare and does not appear to have competed very successfully with the other machines, which all worked on a loom principle with 'bobbins' and produced a net of twisted threads, while the Warp Frame used rows of needles to make its loops.

In the later nineteenth century and early twentieth century the immense variety of patterns which the versatile Levers machine could produce nearly caused Warp Frame lace to die out. However, during the 1920s it revived, producing openwork silk dress laces; and the more recent synthetic fibres were admirably suited to its techniques. It now produces the raschel nets, lace fabrics and narrow edgings which dominate the market, as well as tights, lastex underwear and lightweight curtain material.

The main identifying features of the Warp Frame are:

1. The threads making up the ground or fabric are not twisted but looped.
2. The crossing of the threads from one vertical row to another occurred on the reverse side of the lace, which consequently looked rather muddled at the back while smooth at the front. Other machine laces are sufficiently similar on the two sides to be reversible, though there is more difference than in handmade bobbin laces.
3. The picot edging was always separately attached.
4. There was no strong indication of parallel lines as there was on a Levers lace.

ii. The Bobbin Net machine

This machine twisted the threads to make the net instead of looping them as did the Warp Frame. The first twist-net machine was patented in 1808 by John Heathcoat, then aged twenty-five, in the Midlands. His aim was to produce an imitation ground which could be mistaken for bobbin work, and he succeeded in producing an excellent copy of fond simple. The warp threads were longitudinally stretched on the loom while the weft threads passed across and around them, so that when the net was removed from the loom and the tension released it fell into small hexagonal meshes. It was called bobbin net — sometimes abbreviated to bobbinet, which avoids ambiguity — or 'two-twist net', because in the hexagonal mesh four sides were twisted twice and two sides crossed. The word 'bobbin' refers to the bobbins on the loom, and the word 'net' should always be restricted to a machine product. It was a traversed net, that is the moving threads, as in bobbin lace, passed diagonally, not horizontally, from one side of the lace to the other and back again.

In 1831 a 'three-twist' or 'Brussels' net was invented. In this the mesh was diamond-shaped, with three twists on the four sides, the crossed threads on the remaining two sides being so short as not to affect the shape. This net is no longer made, though the date when its production ceased is not known. Indeed records of what was made by each machine, in what quantities and when, are very difficult, even impossible, to trace. Some old records were destroyed by a fire at the Heathcoat factory in 1931; others in the Midlands seem to have passed into the hands of the owners' families and been thrown away. Research projects attempted by students at Nottingham and other universities have come to nothing through lack of material. Felkin's contemporary nineteenth-century account is invaluable, but there has been nothing, in detail, to follow on from where his chronicle ends.

Bobbinet of the two-twist variety is still manufactured at the Heathcoat factory in Tiverton, and between 1970 and 1979 the approximate quantities produced in various threads were: nylon 4 million square metres; silk 250,000; elastic 100,000; while the production in cotton was minimal. Much of this net was exported, in particular to Japan. Very recently production of silk bobbinet has ceased.

The productions of the Bobbin Net machine can be distinguished from handmade bobbin laces by:

1. Wide pieces without joins could be made, after 1809, while the lacemaker's pillow enables only narrow strips to be produced.
2. The three-twist net has no handmade equivalent.
3. The decoration of bobbinet was by some form of embroidery or by appliqué work. In each case the net continued through the design, while in handwork the reseau stopped at the toilé. If the embroidery was tambour work, chain stitches would be identified; if it was needlerun, the thread would be seen going in and out of the meshes.
4. The picot was machine-made and then stitched on, while in bobbin lace the picot threads were continuous with the main fabric.

Heathcoat's Bobbin Net machine seldom produced any machine-patterned laces: it used two layers of bobbins and therefore could not be adapted to the Jacquard apparatus. However, it has a place in this section since both the Pusher and Levers machines, famous for their mid nineteenth-century patterned laces, began by producing a twisted traversed net similar to Heathcoat's, before technical modifications made them distinctive.

iii. The Pusher machine

The Pusher Machine, invented in 1812, produced in its early days only a holey openwork lace, sometimes similar to a bobbin-made honeycomb design. It could also make a close imitation of the wholestitch and halfstitch of bobbin laces and in many cases the picot edging, though in larger pieces this had usually to be separately attached. After the application of the Jacquard apparatus in the 1840s its imitations of the Chantilly laces were uncannily exact, and often the only way to be certain that a lace is machine-made and not handmade is to examine the cordonnet, which the Pusher never mastered and which had therefore always to be run in by hand.

Pusher laces reached the height of their popularity in the 1860s, when crinolines were in fashion, and its most striking examples were the so-

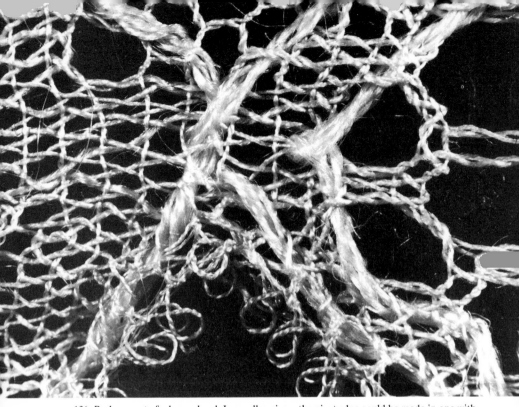

136. Pusher: part of a large shawl. In smaller pieces the picot edge could be made in one with the rest, but in large pieces it was separately attached. Here the binding stitches can be seen, though not clearly because the thread is well matched. Note the needlerun cordonnet. (13 mm.)

called Lama laces, large shawls or capes of mohair, where the springy fibre produced in the ground even the slight irregularity of a handmade reseau.

Production of Pusher laces ceased in the 1870s.

iv. The Levers machine

The Levers machine was invented in 1813, and early modifications resulted in bobbins and carriages so thin that they could be mounted in a single tier, and Jacquard cards could be used to control the sideways movement of the guide bars through which the warp threads passed to form the pattern. The weft or bobbin threads in these laces remained stationary, while the warp or beam threads were manipulated around them, producing in the more solid parts a kind of zigzag effect (fig. 137). This effect is clearly visible with a magnifier and is quite different from the more smoothly woven appearance of Pusher machine, and of hand-made bobbin, laces.

By the mid nineteenth century the Levers machine was producing

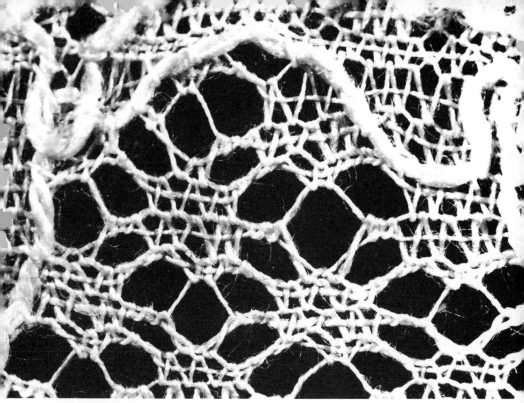

137. Levers: a piece 13 mm long, showing both the typical zigzag effect of the beam thread, passing between the bobbin threads and helping to strengthen their ridged effect, and the cordonnet, attached to the front of the lace by threads going from the design to the ground.

imitations of every kind of handmade bobbin lace — whether Mechlin, Valenciennes, Bucks, Cluny, Maltese or Honiton — and most could be distinguished from the real thing only with difficulty. 'Spanish laces' in the form of heavy black edging, the designs imitating those of Spanish bobbin, were made in huge quantities in the 1880s.

In all this variety a number of distinctive features remained clear:

1. The zigzag or V-shaped movement of threads in the toilé.
2. The strong impression of parallel lines or ridges running lengthwise in the lace. This was emphasised partly by the twisting of the warps around the stretched longitudinal threads and partly by the use of thinner weft threads, which sharpened the contrast.
3. The threads did not pass diagonally, that is the lace was not traversed.
4. The cordonnet, from 1841, could be put in quite skilfully by machine, even to the extent of being enclosed by threads passing between the design and ground in a manner similar to bobbin laces, though a good deal less neatly. In Levers lace this cordonnet often, though not invariably, lies on one side of the lace, giving the appearance of a raised

138. Levers: part of a lappet of imitation Mechlin design. The copy is very convincing, but the cordonnet is attached to one side only, giving a raised front (on the right) and a flat back (on the left); and the reseau is quite rigidly regular. (240 mm.)

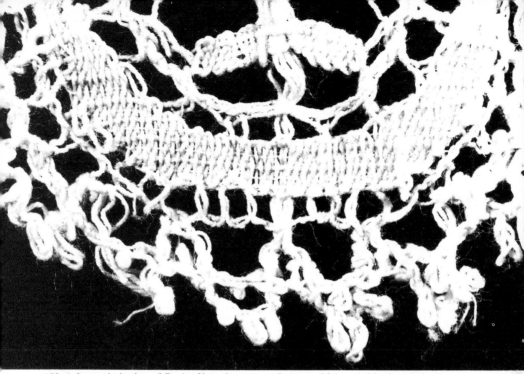

139. A Levers imitation of Bucks. Note the contrast between thick and thin threads in the toilé and, in the looser parts, the thin threads appearing to bind the thicker ones together. The picot is made in one with the lace but it is, under magnification, very awkwardly done. (25 mm.)

140. A bobbin lace of somewhat similar design to 139. Note that the threads from lace to picot and back, and over and under the cordonnet, are sharp and clear, and they can also be traced in and out of the corners of the tallies. (13 mm.)

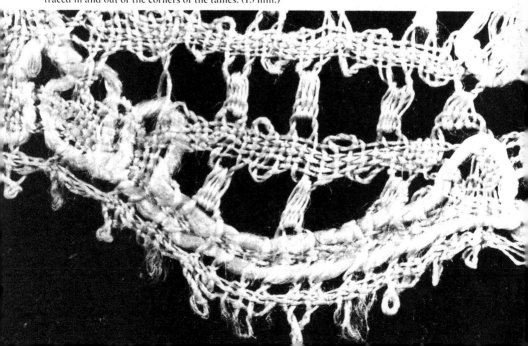

front and a flat back, which is different from both a Warp Frame and a handmade bobbin lace. This invention put an end to the employment of 'lace runners', who had darned in the cordonnet, and frequently also the design, before 1840. Thus Warp Frame and Levers laces with a needlerun cordonnet antedate the 1850s. A handrun cordonnet can be distinguished not only by the neat ducking in and out of the threads through the meshes, but also by the fact that each thread has just two cuts in it, at the beginning and end of each outline, while a machine cordonnet has four cuts, since two separate patterning threads are needed to go around either side of the design.

5. In the second half of the nineteenth century the Levers machine could make a picot edge continuous with the fabric, though some hand-finishing might be needed and the result was not always very tidy.

The variety of laces produced by the Levers machines in the nineteenth century seems almost limitless, and if you try to collect machine laces you will probably find that over 90 per cent of those you come across will be Levers. Its real excellence lay in its superb imitations of bobbin laces, which were able to save the upper classes a great deal of money. However, with the end of the Victorian era the social need for everything at least to appear handmade became outmoded and designs more in keeping with an increasingly machine-orientated world had to be invented. Thus Levers lost its greatest advantage. Compared with the revitalised Warp Frame and another machine called the Barmen shortly to be described, it was ponderous, slow and costly, and its popularity has waned steadily until it is now in danger of ceasing production.

v. The Lace Curtain machine

The Lace Curtain machine was also developed from a traversed twist net machine, but a modification of 1846 enabled it to make a patterned lace which was not traversed. Basically it remained similar to Levers in that it was the warp threads which moved to produce the pattern and the longitudinal parallel lines stood out sharply in the finished lace. However, it was coarser, less durable and less flexible in design. One of its most distinctive features was the rigid square mesh produced by the spacing of the V-shaped connections. It was used only for large pieces.

vi. The Barmen machine

The Barmen machine was invented early in the twentieth century but did not come into general use until the 1920s or 1930s. It was derived from a flat braider and uses a weaving technique, so that its simple edgings of coarse thread are indistinguishable from handmade torchon or Cluny except for an inhuman regularity of aspect. It is used for edgings and insertions up to about 4 inches (100 millimetres) wide.

141. Lace Curtain machine, twentieth century. Note the shaded patterning, the strong parallel lines and the square mesh. (200 mm.)
142. Lace Curtain machine: a close-up of the square mesh. (20 mm.)

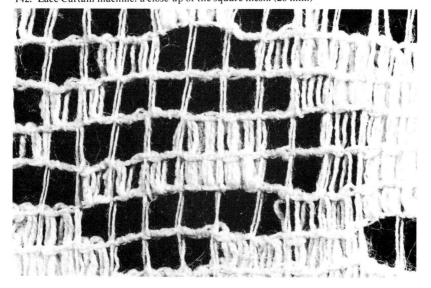

Summary of the distinctive features of machine laces

1. There is often a longitudinal ribbed effect, which may be more clearly visible if the lace is held up to the light.
2. The picot edging may be separately attached or, if continuous with the main fabric, untidily finished.
3. The cordonnet, if put in by machine, shows two cut ends at the beginning of the motif and two more at the end of it since the machine cannot move backwards to complete the perimeter of the shape, and two cordonnet threads have to be used.
4. The back and front of the lace are sometimes different.
5. Machine lace is made from cotton, wool, silk or nylon, but not flax.
6. There may be a frequent contrast between thicker and thinner threads in the toilé, with the thinner threads appearing to bind the thicker ones together.
7. The footing of bobbin lace is more uneven than the rigid machine copy; also it can be gathered by pulling the footing thread. So can the Barmen, but other machine laces cannot.

The deliberate imitation of handmade techniques by the machines, particularly in the mid nineteenth century, does not make identification easy. Sometimes a machine net was edged with a picot made by bobbins. Conversely, an eighteenth-century bobbin lace might have a nineteenth-century machine picot attached around it, perhaps because its own edge was damaged. Even fake joins were sometimes faintly run in on a machine net to make it look as though it had been made up of narrow strips, as a bobbin lace would be.

All these machines used a modified weaving process and so could imitate only bobbin laces, not needlepoint ones. However, needlepoint ones were imitated and this, as one might expect, was by a modified embroidery process producing 'chemical lace'.

Chemical lace

This was invented in 1883, as a development of machine embroidery, and the technique was perfected in Switzerland and Germany at about the same time. The embroidery was worked in cotton on a background of silk, and the silk was then dissolved away by a corrosive such as chlorine or caustic soda. Hence the names 'chemical', 'burnt' or 'Swiss' lace. This technique was used to great effect to imitate almost every lace that has ever existed, from sixteenth-century cutwork, reticella and punto in aria to nineteenth-century Brussels Duchesse, Point de Gaz, Irish crochet and even Honiton. The most obvious point of identification is in the fuzziness of the brides, and indeed a kind of scrambled look to all the threads if examined under the magnifier. No clear stitches can be seen, nor can the course of the individual threads be followed.

143. Chemical lace, late nineteenth century. Note the fuzziness of all the lines, an important diagnostic feature. This is not obvious from a distance. (110 mm.)

144. Chemical lace embroidered on two-twist net, with some cloth appliqué to make a superficial resemblance to Point de Gaz. Again the extreme fuzziness of the threads and the inability to distinguish either a bobbin or needlepoint technique indicate a machine origin. (110 mm.)

So finally, another method of distinguishing handmade and machine-made laces is: in handmade it is always possible to see how it was made; the twisting or plaiting of threads in bobbin lace should be clearly visible, and so should the buttonhole stitches of needlepoint. Any fuzziness or looped-over appearance is an indication of machine manufacture. But there is no easy way to expertise, and the early stages need a lot of patience and a lot of practice: the eye must be trained so that it knows what to look for, and the mind so that it correctly interprets what is seen.

The machine laces, though not entirely responsible in themselves for the decline of handmade laces, certainly made existence very difficult for them since they could not be produced quickly enough to compete commercially with the products of the looms. Attempts to produce lace-like textiles with the object of bringing in a little income for the individual worker, combined with the popularity of amateur crafts in the late nineteenth and early twentieth centuries, led to what I have called, for want of a better word, imitation laces.

(c) IMITATION LACES

Most of these were not new techniques but were based on old forms, revived in the 1840s and 1850s, often using some implement such as a needle, hook or shuttle.

i. Filet

Filet, or lacis, has been discussed already under sixteenth-century embroidered laces, and it reappears here only because of its popularity among amateur embroiderers from Victorian times to the present day. The hand-knotted, square or diamond-shaped mesh, made with fishernet knots using a netting shuttle and mesh stick, could be bought ready-made and fixed to a metal frame. The pattern was then worked using a darning stitch, the technique for this remaining unchanged through five centuries. Occasionally a plain knotted ground was used for curtains. Small mats, decorated with cupids or classical profiles, are still made in Italy as tourist pieces, some using old Vinciolo designs.

ii. Knitting

Though some of this dates from Regency times, knitted lace was typically a Victorian time filler for leisured ladies. It was used to make bed covers and to trim towels and tablecloths as well as clothes. Some gossamer-fine knitting, known as Pita lace, was produced in the Azores, usually in the form of small mats with ornamental centres. The thread used was fibre from the century plant. The light openwork shawls of Shetland wool, fine enough to pass through a wedding ring, can also be regarded as a form of lace. The implements were knitting needles, varying

145. A knitted mat: Pita lace from the Azores. (120 mm.)

in number from one to four; the technique was the making of horizontal rows of loops from a continuous thread.

iii. Knotted lace

This was made in the Middle East, for example Syria and Palestine, Armenia and Algeria. It could be produced as edging or as tiny rosettes which were made up into collars or bonnets. A needle similar to a sewing needle was used in the knotting of the thread.

iv. Netting

The materials used in this craft varied from fine string to silk or even chenille, but in all the technique was basically the same. A netting shuttle holding a measured length of thread was used, and the mesh was kept of constant size by a mesh stick of wood or steel. The basic knot was similar to the weaver's knot used in weaving and bookbinding, also called the sheet bend when used in sailing. Many netted miser's purses were produced in the nineteenth century.

146 (top left). Knotted lace from the Mediterranean area, either Cyprus or the Middle East. (80 mm.)
147 (bottom left). Netting, from a miser's purse. (9 mm.)
148 (below). Macramé: the long tassels are characteristic, being the remainder of measured lengths of thread. (330 mm.)

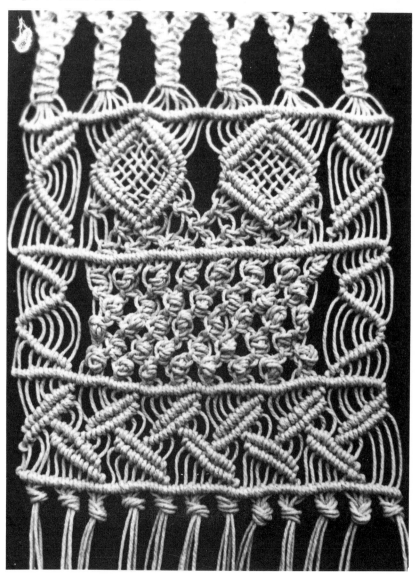

v. Macramé

Macramé differed technically from knotted lace in that the knots were made by hand instead of with a needle, and also that several lengths of thread had first to be cut to a suitable size; it differed from netting in both the method of working and the type of knot. A holding cord was first fastened to a firm surface, then the pre-cut lengths were fixed to it by a reversed double half hitch so that two ends of equal length hung down. One of these lengths then acted as a support or knot-bearing cord, while the other, the knotting cord, was tied around it. The basic knots were the half hitch and the flat knot, but there were many variations. In Victorian times macramé was used for the fringing of antimacassars, doyleys and shawls, but it is one of the very oldest types of lace, a precursor of bobbin, and known in the sixteenth century as *punto a groppo*. It has enjoyed a number of revivals, including a current one begun in the USA. The modern products are usually coarse wall hangings or pot holders, but there are patterns available for belts, sweaters, rugs or lampshades.

vi. Tatting

Though this certainly dates from the eighteenth century, and possibly earlier, it declined greatly in popularity and did not revive until about 1850, when Mlle Riego published several volumes of instructions and designs and won four awards at the International Exhibition. Tatting consists of tying knots either in circles or along a foundation thread, using a tatting shuttle. Unlike macramé it uses basically only one knot, the lark's head or cow hitch, made up of two half hitches, each a mirror image of the other. Loops of thread left between the knots form picots, which can be of varying length and frequency. Also unlike macramé, it uses a continuous thread. Many innovations of design and technique came from Queen Marie of Rumania. An expert tatter, she worked large ecclesiastical pieces and spangled them with topaz, turquoise, pearl and crystal jewels. Subsequently she donated them to the monastery of Sinaia in the Carpathians in order, it is said, that her precious stones should not fall into the clutches of her husband's mistress.

vii. Spanish Wheel

Spanish Ruedas or Wheel design, sometimes known as Sun Lace, was worked in a similar way to Teneriffe lace. The general technique was to make a circle of about fifty-two pins, pass cotton threads as diameters between them, and then to make a pattern of concentric circles using a needle and thread. A more dexterous lace, made in natural-coloured silk, was Nanduti. This came from Paraguay and consisted of a rayed foundation which was later decorated in a great variety of ways. It was very laborious to make, but the results were quite breathtaking. A similar

149. Tatting: the basic unit of circles, or ovals, with picots, combined into an attractive antimacassar. Late nineteenth century. (190 mm.)
150. Spanish Wheel design combined with needle-weaving. (180 mm.)

151. Tenerife work: a small piece inserted into a cloth. (80 mm.)
152. Nanduti: the silk border of a handkerchief. It is basically similar to 150 and 151 in its rayed design but much more skilled and varied. (250 mm to edge of lace.)

lace, made in Mexico, was called Tucuman. Paraguay, Mexico and Tenerife had all been influenced by Spanish domination.

viii. Chinese drawn work

This was similar in general appearance to the Sun laces but was based on a finely woven cotton or on pina cloth made from the fibres of the pineapple plant. The threads in one direction were removed and those in the other direction were bound together and overstitched in pairs to form a design, a process sometimes known as needle-weaving. Another kind of decorative drawn work was made in the Philippines.

ix. Crochet

Crochet, made with a crochet hook and using cotton thread, was, like knitting, most commonly an amateur product. It was used as a decoration for household linen and also for cotton nightdresses, chemises and petticoats. Pretty designs did exist, but many were unimaginative. More interesting were the cot covers and wall hangings depicting biblical scenes, such as Daniel in the Lion's Den, or Aesop's Fables, for example the Fox and the Grapes. It is said to have developed from tambour work.

153. Crochet: part of a mitten. The stitches and designs are distinctive. (90 mm.)

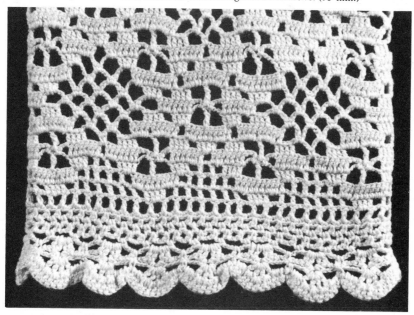

x. Irish crochet

Irish crochet, also worked with a crochet hook, but often an extremely thin-hooked steel one, is in a class by itself. It was first produced in the mid 1840s, and the earlier pieces were of fine thread and closely textured workmanship, producing good imitations in appearance of Venetian Gros Point and Coralline. In the later nineteenth century, as with the other hand laces, production was hurried, and designs became careless and the work loose and ill formed. Large clumsy motifs were joined by bars of coarse meshworks, or poor-quality thread was used for layered rose petals, monotonously scattered over a flimsy base. This rather mechanical Irish crochet was extensively copied in India and in Australia to make collars and tablemats. The best Irish crochet has a grandeur all its own, but it is not easy to find. The material was mainly cotton, but silk was occasionally used.

xi. 'Point' lace

'Point' lace was a highly misleading term for a popular diversion of the second half of the nineteenth century and the early twentieth, and it has already been referred to on page 46 under the name of Renaissance lace because of its imitation of the seventeenth- and eighteenth-century Italian tape laces, which it initially attempted to resemble. It was worked by amateurs rather than commercially, using machine braid or tape, twisted to follow the lines of a pattern printed or inked on to cotton, the various curves and convolutions then being filled with a variety of needlemade stitches and linked by brides worked over with buttonhole stitch. Different designs carried names such as Point de Venise, Honiton Point and Battenburg. They can look extremely effective from a distance, whether worn as dress decoration or used to trim table covers, but on the whole the workmanship was very slight. Branscombe was probably the finest and most skilfully worked form, and its technique is now being revived. A considerable variety of shapes of tape could be bought, and they were sometimes linked by crochet instead of by needlepoint brides. Not all the designs were derivative: some were original and of an art nouveau type.

xii. Whitework

Whitework, though not a lace in the usual sense, will be mentioned here because it often employed cutwork and needlepoint techniques. The two most important holey varieties were Ayrshire work and broderie anglaise.

Ayrshire work originated from the Dresden work of the second half of the eighteenth century. This was made first of all on very thin linen, but by

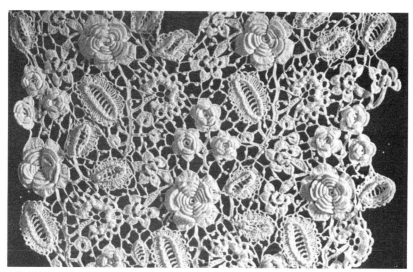

154. Irish crochet. The tiered rose petals and picoted brides are typical of fine-quality work. The design is often imitative — here it copies Honiton to some extent. (150 mm.)

155 'Point' (Renaissance) lace. Above is the pattern with the machine tape tacked in position, some of the guide lines for the buttonhole-stitch filling put in and some of the ground worked. Below is a completed portion of the lace detached from its pattern. (190 mm.)

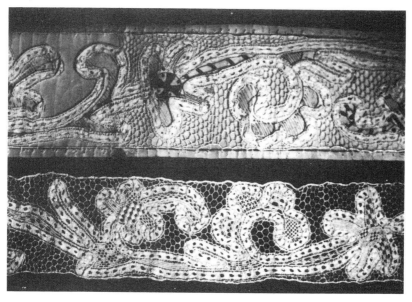

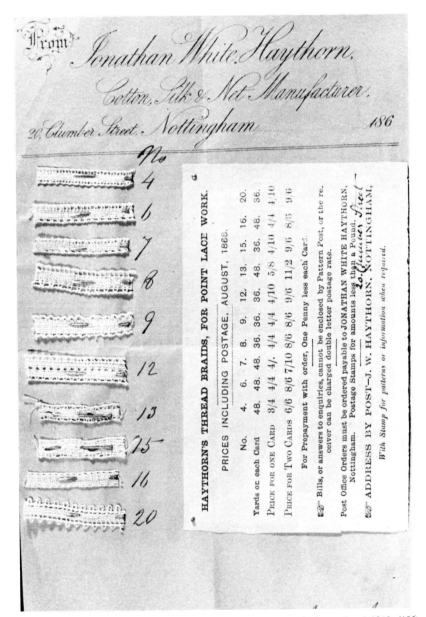

156. Samples of tapes for point lace work from Haythorn, Nottingham, dated 1868. (180 mm.)

157. Part of an Ayrshire work design: the centre of the flower has been completely cut out, then filled with buttonhole stitching. (50 mm.)

the 1780s fine Dacca or Indian muslins, said to be so sheer that eleven thicknesses were still translucent, were in vogue, and it was the height of fashion to wear a simple white muslin gown, with muslin cap and cotton stockings. Scottish weavers, obtaining a fine thread from the textile mills at Manchester, copied these Indian muslins with great success, and they were encouraged to do this by an import levy of 18 per cent against the Indian products. An Italian, Luigi Ruffini, settled in Edinburgh and concerned himself with the decoration of these muslins. The decoration was at first by chainstitch or pulled thread embroidery, using a supporting tambour, or wooden hoop, with the design drawn on a card held beneath the material. From simple dots and sprigs the designs became more elaborate, and the industry prospered. By 1802 import duties had risen to 31 per cent, by 1813 to 44 per cent and by 1816 Scotland was exporting muslin to India. Experiments in the machine-weaving of muslin were made around 1800, but hand-weaving continued until 1820.

It was against this background that Ayrshire work began. In 1814 Lady Montgomerie of Eglinton brought back from France a baby robe which had been embroidered there. The stitches of this were analysed and then copied by a Mrs Jamieson. The earliest examples of this work were on cotton muslin, and then on fine cambric or lawn. On baby gowns the front of the bodice and skirt were profusely decorated with an abundance of small flowers and trailing foliage. In slightly later, and perhaps less expensive, gowns the decoration was sometimes rather sparse, but particularly characteristic were the sprigs like tiny thistles which bordered the neck, sleeves and edging around the bodice and skirt panels. The centres of the flowers were decorated with minute ornamental fillings. In the first place this was done by pulled threadwork as in the parental Dresden; later the small shapes were completely removed and then the holes in the cloth filled in either with needlepoint stitches in various designs or with plain net or with net darned over with needlerun in the manner of the most delicate Limerick work.

In the 1820s and 1830s Ayrshire work was very popular for pelerines, cuffs, flounces and caps. However, the era of muslin was almost over, and during the second half of the nineteenth century both the white material and its embroidery tended to become coarser.

Broderie anglaise. In this the pattern was drawn or stencilled on to a firm cotton material. The holes were punched out, tacked around for firmness and then oversewn, often by professionals for a commercial market. Occasionally in more amateur work the holes were formed with a stiletto or even cut out with scissors after the stitching had been done. Vast quantities of this type of edging and insertion exist, some made in England and

158. Broderie anglaise: a design for a cuff punched out ready for embroidery. (200 mm.)

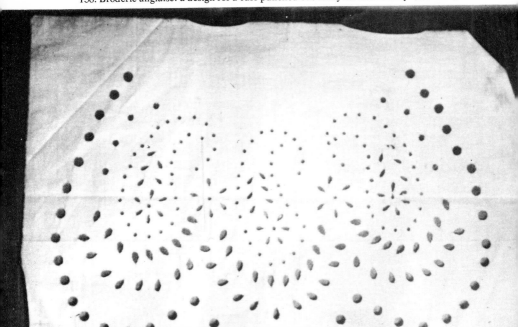

159. Swiss embroidery: part of an edging worked by machine, the reverse side, showing the extremely close resemblance of the stitching and finishing to handwork. Often it is indistinguishable except by the mechanical precision of the repeat. (100 mm.)

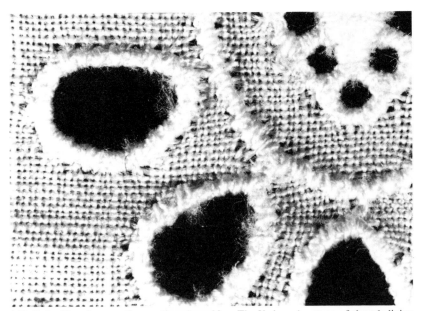

160. Embroidery by a continuous thread machine. The V-shaped pattern of threads lining the holes and forming the oval is quite unlike handwork. (110 mm.)

161. Richelieu work: the stitching is around the outside of the design, not binding the holes, as in broderie anglaise; also the holes are cut after the stitching is done so that the finish is less neat. (140 mm.)

some in Madeira, but in most the design is rigid and repetitive. They had little artistic advantage over the completely machine-made white embroidery produced in Switzerland from about 1870 onwards and known as Swiss embroidery.

Swiss embroidery. This was made on a pantograph, with numerous needles using a limited length of thread and doing exactly the same work as one held by hand, and the finish of satin, stem and overcast stitches was indistinguishable. However, the machine could not produce a knotting stitch, nor could it avoid the short mechanical-looking repeat.

For example, if the reverse of the work is examined it can be seen that ıthe thread passing from one small part of the design to another has each time an identical point of entry and exit, and also that the number of stitches per stem, leaf or petal is invariably the same, which would not happen in handwork.

A less refined form of machine whitework or broderie anglaise used a continuous thread, and the zigzagging of the stitches around the punched holes bears no resemblance to hand embroidery.

xiii. Richelieu work

Though more of an embroidery than a lace, this appears nevertheless something like a bobbin guipure. Whereas in broderie anglaise it is the holes which are stitched around, in Richelieu work it is the solid parts, usually flowers and leaves, which have a stitched border, and they are then linked by brides before the intervening material is cut away. Thus it has some similarity in technique to a Carrickmacross guipure, though the motifs are bordered with embroidery stitching and not by an oversewn outlining thread.

The decadence and loss of lace in its complex artistic forms will be for ever a matter for regret, but it is to be hoped that this brief account will enable you to identify all that is good and valuable both financially and as a relic of human endeavour, and so to save from destruction, care for and preserve whatever remains of the antique laces.

COMPARISON OF LACE MACHINE
AND BOBBIN LACE PRODUCTS

type of lace	traversed	picot	cordonnet	mesh	comment
Warp Frame	No	Stitched on separately	Handrun till the 1840s, then made by machine.	Made up of vertical rows of loops, each using a separate thread, but anchoring across from one row to another.	Now produces raschel lace, developed for nets, dress laces, edgings and underwear.
Bobbin Net machine	Yes	Stitched on separately	Not usually any machine patterning, could be needlerun.	Weft threads twisted diagonally across and around warp forming two-twist or three-twist net.	Synthetic thread now used, and three-twist no longer made.
Pusher machine	Yes	Continuous with the fabric in smaller pieces, separate in bigger.	Always handrun.	Formed by movement of weft threads, producing hexagonal or honeycomb mesh. No strong ribbing.	Production stopped about 1870.
Levers machine	No	Stitched on separately at first, later continuous.	By machine after 1840, but more prominent on the front of the lace.	Pattern produced by movement of warp threads. Often strong ribbing. Many types of bobbin reseau imitated.	Too slow for modern production — the winding of thread on the bobbins very tedious. Declining.
Lace Curtain machine	No	Continuous with the fabric.	Machine.	Pattern produced by movement of warp threads. Typical large square mesh.	Produced large pieces of lace only. To some extent superseded by raschel lace curtains.
Bucks bobbin lace	Yes	The threads passing from toilé to picot and back are clear, neat and uncut.	Enclosed by clear threads passing between the toilé and the reseau.	Hexagonal fond simple, very similar to two-twist bobbin net.	Maximum width about 4ins (100mm). Larger pieces had to be joined.

GLOSSARY

Alb flounce: a fairly deep (8-12 inches, 200-300mm) flounce of lace attached to the hem or lower part of a priest's alb.

Altar frontal: the lace or embroidered material passing along the front and sides of an altar.

Appliqué lace: sprigs or motifs attached to a continuous background of machine net or, rarely, bobbin reseau. The motifs may be of bobbin, needlepoint or muslin.

Bertha: a collar 4-8 inches (100-200mm) deep and a yard or more (1 metre) long, worn on a décolleté dress.

Blonde lace: a silk lace, whether white or black. Originally used of a natural-coloured as opposed to a bleached silk, but then of any silk lace. This led to linguistic contortions such as black blonde, white blonde and blonde silk.

Bobbin: the elongated bone or wood weights on which the thread is wound in bobbin lace and which provide tension; also the shuttles used in weaving, particularly on hand looms.

Bone lace: an early name for bobbin lace.

Brides, bars, bridges: narrow bobbin or needlemade threads linking the individually made motifs of a lace design.

Brides picotées: brides decorated with tiny loops.

Cordonnet, trolly, gimp: an outline of the motifs of lace, made either of single thread (gimp) or of several strands, or of a padded wreath oversewn with buttonhole stitch.

Cotton: the cellulose floss surrounding the seeds of the cotton plant, when it has been separated from the seeds and spun into threads. The threads when woven produce a 'cotton material'.

Cravat: a neckcloth rather like a linen scarf, the ends (about 8 inches, 200 mm, square) being made of bobbin or needlepoint lace, often of elaborate design.

Drawn threadwork: a form of punto tirato in which individual threads are removed from the material in making the embroidered design.

Droschel, vrai reseau: a term restricted to the Flemish reseau, a hexagonal mesh with two sides of four threads plaited four times and four sides of two threads twisted twice.

Ecru: a French term for raw silk or the colour of unbleached linen, hence a material dipped in tea or coffee to achieve that colour.

Edging: a narrow lace trimming of which one side only is attached to the material.

Engageants: cuffs fashionable in the eighteenth century, about 2 feet (600 mm) long and with an asymmetrical border, made to be tightly gathered and stitched to the sleeve end.

Fillings, jours, modes: fancy stitchings used to fill enclosed spaces in lace, for example the centres of flowers or leaves.

Flax: see *Linen*.

Flounce, furbelow: a widish edging (often used of any edging more than 4 inches, 100mm, wide), usually gathered or pleated at the footing.

Fontange: an exaggeratedly high head decoration of lace, fashionable around 1700.

Footside, footing: the straight side of lace edging or flouncing, which is attached to the material in wear.

Gimp: originally a lace made without bobbins or needle, in the seventeenth century; also a heavy thread passing through the centre of a bobbin trail, or around the outer border, in which case it is known as a cordonnet; a gimp or trolly bobbin is the bobbin which carries this heavy thread.

Greek lace: a name used for cutwork and reticella.

Guipure: originally a lace of narrow parchment tapes whipped round with silk or gold or silver thread; thence a lace made of bobbin or woven tapes filled with bobbin or needle stitches and linked by brides; thence any lace where the parts of the toilé are joined by brides.

Headside, heading: the free, often scalloped or shaped side of lace edging or flouncing, not attached to the material in wear.

Insertion: a length of lace in which the two borders are the same and both are attached to the material in wear.

Jabot: a decorative neck frill, attached to a blouse, dress or shirt at the base of the throat.

Lappets: hanging strips of lace 2-4 inches (50-100mm) wide and of variable length, attached to the sides of the head, i.e. they were made in pairs.

Lawn: a fine translucent linen or cotton material.

Linen: a material woven from the bast fibres in the stem of the flax plant. The separation of the fibres from the other tissues of the stem, before the spinning into thread can begin, is a lengthy process and adds to the expense of linen as compared with cotton. The fibres are of cellulose reinforced with lignin and therefore stronger, smoother, firmer and cooler than cotton, which is pure cellulose.

Muslin: a translucent cotton material.

Needlepoint, needle lace: lace built up entirely of buttonhole stitches.

Net: a machine-made mesh; but 'net' is also used in modern lacemaking, e.g. net-stitch (Honiton), and net-ground (Bucks). To avoid ambiguity in the text I have used the somewhat tautological term 'machine net'.

Pelerine: used of an early nineteenth-century deep collar, almost like a short cape, usually of muslin with white embroidery.

Picots, pearls: short loops used to enrich the brides or the outline of the toilé; also a narrow edge of projecting loops along the heading, made either by hand or by machine.

Pillow lace: often used as synonymous with bobbin lace, but ambiguous since needlepoint lace frequently also used the support of a pillow.

Plaits: used in the sense of the ordinary plaiting of threads; but see also *Point d'esprit.*

Point d'esprit, spots, dots, leadworks, plaits, tallies: small square or diamond-shaped decorations of closely worked basket stitch or spot stitch, often regularly arranged through the reseau, for example in Lille. Tallies is a Bucks word for this type of decoration. The four threads which make the point d'esprit come in at each corner of the square or rectangle so that the ends cannot be pointed. Occasionally the entire background is formed of these square-ended plaits, as in some Honiton edging and in so called Beds Plaited lace. See fig. 140. See also *Wheatears.*

Point lace: an abbreviation of needlepoint lace; used also of any fine-quality lace; and of the late nineteenth-century tape laces which imitated the designs of the early needlepoints.

Pricking: the marking out of a pattern on a card or parchment used for bobbin work, the design being pierced in outline by a pricker to receive the pins.

Pulled threadwork, drawn fabric: a form of punto tirato in which the individual threads are pulled together in a great variety of ways to make the design.

Punto tagliato: cutwork.

Rabat: a broad flat collar fitting around the base of the throat and stretching across the shoulders and to some extent over the back and chest.

Raccroc: a stitch used to join invisibly strips of droschel.

Regrounding: replacement of the original background reseau either in whole or in part with a similar reseau, with a different reseau, or by machine net, which is then cut away behind the toilé. When the net is continuous behind the toilé this is referred to as appliqué work.

Reseau, mesh, fond, ground: the background of a lace design, made either in one with the toilé, as in many bobbin laces, or made afterwards to link the pieces of toilé into some form of design, as in needlepoint laces.

Ruff: an outstanding collar, usually several inches deep, and kept stiff by starching.

Silk: a thread and material of animal origin, as opposed to flax and cotton, which come from plants. Silk comes from protein fibres forming the cocoon around the chrysalis of various moths. As in linen, the preparation of the fibres for spinning takes time and care, increasing the cost of the material.

Spangles: the glass beads hung on bobbins, especially those of the Midlands, to increase the weight. There are no spangles on Downton or Honiton bobbins.

Tallies: see *Point d'esprit.*

Toilé: the pattern or clothlike portion in both bobbin and needlepoint laces. In bobbin laces a distinction is made between the closer cloth-work (wholestitch) and the looser openwork (halfstitch) of the toilé.

Traversed net: a form originally invented by Heathcoat in 1808 in which the weft threads pass diagonally across and around the warp, thus producing a close imitation of bobbin fond simple, where the threads are also worked in a diagonal manner.

Trolly lace: basically any bobbin lace where the toilé is outlined with a single-thread cordonnet, but usually used of coarse laces made all in one piece in Devon or the Midlands. Some authorities favour the use of trolly and guipure to cover the two basic bobbin techniques: trolly laces for all those where the toilé and reseau are made together in continuity; and guipure laces for all those where the toilé is made separately and then linked by brides or reseau. Though convenient, this definition is not in general acceptance.

Tulle: silk net.

Warp and Weft: in fabrics, the longitudinally stretched threads on a loom, and the threads worked transversely across them. In machine laces the distinction is less sharp: in Levers and Lace Curtain machines it is the warp threads which are worked around the weft, while in traversed nets and Pusher laces the weft threads move, but diagonally instead of straight across.

Wheatears, leaves, fat, Maltese petals, seeds, grains and paddles: decorations of closely worked basket stitch, often forming an important part of the design, as in Genoese, Maltese Beds and Le Puy. They differ from *Point d'esprit (q.v.)* in being elongated and pointed since the four threads from which they are made come together in pairs at each end. (See fig. 116.)

Wool: an animal fibre, a form of hair, made from keratin and with a slightly scaly surface.

BIBLIOGRAPHY

Cave, Oenone. *Linen Cut-work*. Vista Books, 1963.
Downton Lace Industry. Downton (Salisbury) Museum, Wilts, 1961.
Druk, Derde. *Kant*. Rijksmuseum, Amsterdam, 1966.
Felkin, W. *History of the Machine-wrought Hosiery and Lace Manufacturers*. David and Charles, 1967.
Goubaud, Madame. *Pillow Lace Patterns*. Ward, Lock and Tyler, n.d.
Halls, Zillah. *Machine-made Lace in Nottingham*. The City of Nottingham Museum and Libraries Committee, 1973.
Hawkins, Daisy Waterhouse. *Old Point Lace*. Chatto and Windus, 1878.
Henneberg, F.A. von. *The Art and Craft of Old Lace*. Batsford, 1931.
Holdgate, Charles. *Netmaking for All*. Mills and Boon, 1970.
Hudson Moore, N. *The Lace Book*. Chapman and Hall, 1905.
Hungerford Pollen, Mrs J. *Seven Centuries of Lace*. Heinemann, 1908.
Inder, P.M. *Honiton Lace*. Exeter Museum Publication, no. 55, 1971.
Jourdain, M. *Old Lace*. Batsford, 1908.
Lefebure, E. *Embroidery and Lace*. Grevel, 1888.
Lowes, Mrs E.L. *Chats on Old Lace and Needlework*. London, 1908.
Luton Museum. *Pillow Lace of the East Midlands*.
May, F.L. *Hispanic Lace and Lace-making*. The Hispanic Society of America, 1939.
Meulen-Nulle, L.W. van der. *Lace*. Merlin Press, London, 1963.
Mincoff, E. and Marriage, M.S. *Pillow Lace*. John Murray, 1907.
Nevill Jackson, Mrs F. *A History of Hand-made Lace*. L. Upcott Gill, London, 1900.
Palliser, Mrs Bury. *History of Lace*. Sampson Low, 1910.
Penderell Moody, A. *Devon Pillow Lace*. Cassell, 1907.
Pond, Gabrielle. *An Introduction to Lace*. Garnstone Press, 1973.
Prickett, Elizabeth. 'Ruskin Lace'. *Lace* no. 8, October 1977; and no. 10, April 1978.
Ricci, Elisa. *Antiché Trine Italiane* (2 volumes). Bergamot, 1911.
Sharp, Mary (A.M.S.). *Point and Pillow Lace*. John Murray, 1913.
Vinciolo, Frederico. *Renaissance Patterns for Lace, Embroidery and Needlepoint*. Dover Publications, New York, 1971.
Vogue Guide to Macramé. Collins, 1972.
Wardle, P. *Victorian Lace*. Herbert Jenkins, 1968.
Whiting, Gertrude. *A Lace Guide for Makers and Collectors*. E. P. Dutton & Co., 1920.
Wright, Doreen. *Bobbin Lace Making*. George Bell and Sons, 1971.
Wright, Thomas. *The Romance of the Lace Pillow*. Armstrong, 1919.

INDEX

Numbers in italic refer to pages with illustrations.